The Single Mom Challenge

Rebuilding your faith, family,
and a new vision for your future

Laura Polk

Lost Sock Publishing

The Single Mom Challenge
Laura Polk

Lost Sock Publishing
Laurinburg, North Carolina 28352

First published in the United States of America by Lost Sock Publishing

Copyright © 2018 by Laura Polk

ISBN-13: 978-1983748134

ISBN-10: 1983748137

Scripture quotations marked (NLT) are taken from the Holy Bible, New Living Translation, copyright ©1996, 2004, 2007, 2013, 2015 by Tyndale House Foundation. Used by permission of Tyndale House Publishers, Inc., Carol Stream, Illinois 60188. All rights reserved.

Scripture quotations marked (NIV) are taken from the Holy Bible, New International Version®,(NIV)®. Copyright © 1973, 1978, 1984, 2011 by Biblica, Inc.™ Used by permission of Zondervan. All rights reserved worldwide. www.zondervan.com The "NIV" and "New International Version" are trademarks registered in the United States Patent and Trademark Office by Biblica, Inc.™

10 9 8 7 6 5 4 3 2 1

www.laurapolk.com

Praise for *The Single Mom Challenge*:

"Every honest parent will tell you they feel inadequate to the task of raising a child. If you're married, at least you have a team member with whom to figure things out. But what if you're a single parent? How do you cover all the bases flying solo?

I'm convinced that single moms can be amazing parents. But the journey is long and challenging; support, encouragement, and a little wisdom from someone who has been there and is doing that is needed. A trusted, fellow journey-woman offering verbal hugs and "you can do its" is worth solid gold when you're in the trenches.

Encouraging a single mom translates into a more emotionally healthy son or daughter who grows to give more to the world than she takes. Inspiring a single mom to follow through in tough moments, fosters spiritual growth in their child. And challenging a single mom to rest in God's provision for her family, reduces anxiety in her children.

The Single Mom Challenge...now this is a good idea."

Ron L. Deal, Speaker, Therapist, and Author of *The Smart Stepfamily* **and** *Dating and the Single Parent*

"Laura Polk, like many single moms, was in a place she never expected to be - parenting alone. While the twists, turns, and unexpected that followed could have been used to claim defeat, Laura is using them as a stepping stone to help others find their victory in Christ Jesus. Praise be to God for the army He is raising up to fight against the lies of the enemy that would have single mothers believe that they could never be used by God."

Jennifer Maggio, Chief Executive Officer, The Life of a Single Mom Ministries, www.thelifeofasinglemom.com

"Wise and witty and gritty and chock full of I'll-walk-with-you encouragement, you'll want to read this book. In The Single Mom Challenge, Laura Polk is raw and honest and makes it feel like joy-filled hope."

Suzanne Eller, author of *Come With Me: Discovering the Beauty of Following Where He Leads*

The Single Mom Challenge is the book I wish I would have had when I was a single mom. With beautiful transparency and well written words of wisdom, Laura Polk leads single moms to embrace their new normal with a passion and purpose that will equip them and their children to not only survive the single parent life, but to thrive in it. *The Single Mom Challenge* is not only a book I would recommend to every single mom on the planet, but it is also a great small group resource as well.

Stephanie Shott, Founder of The MOM Initiative, www.themominitiative.com

"What an amazing tool this book is. Laura Polk's writing is honest and sincere . . . just as her challenges to single moms are thought-provoking and helpful. With Laura at the helm of this unknown territory, single moms everywhere will have not only found a friend, but a mentor to help navigate this season of life."

Jenny Lee Sulpizio, author of *Confessions of a Wonder Woman Wannabe* **and For the** *Love of God*

For all the single moms I've been blessed to walk
alongside in this journey:

This is a sisterhood. You are not in it alone. Accept the
challenge before you and allow God to lead you.
Together with God, we can do anything.

Acknowledgments

A book like this never comes to life by itself. I had a large group of encouragers along my walk:

I would like to thank what I refer to as my "Single Mom Panel", a group of women who agreed early on to interviews and cheered me onward from then until now. Much like them, I want to thank the women who came to contribute through my *The Christian Single Mom* page on Facebook—you are amazing!

Thank you to my dear friend, Becky Roberts, whose wise words kept me on track—when I was smart enough to follow them.

Hugs to Lisa Carpenter, who came as an encourager out of the blue when I was praying daily for an encourager, but in whom I also found a kindred spirit.

Most importantly, sweet praises to Jesus. The One I'd been looking for, the One who never left me (even when I wasn't sure), and the One who gave me a dream for this book and wouldn't let me put it down. I pray that it is used for your glory.

Table of Contents

Chapter 1 Not Where I Want to Be 1

Chapter 2 First Steps 19

Chapter 3 Clinging to the Rock 35

Chapter 4 Addressing the Wound 60

Chapter 5 Rebuilding Yourself 84

Chapter 6 Rebuilding Your Children 101

Chapter 7 Rebuilding with Your Ex...........................125

Chapter 8 Getting Back to Life...........................147

Chapter 9 When You Mess it All Up 174

What Other Single Moms Want You to Know:.........197

Chapter 1

Not Where I Want to Be

{December 30, 2013}

I'm sitting at my computer wearing my new $20 leather boots that I beat off a flurry of women to get on Black Friday. It's two days before the New Year. Two days before the whole world hits restart. One day before loving couples kiss to luck.

And I'm not where I want to be.

For me, the thought of a New Year sounds good. Great actually. We can all stand a little starting over, can't we? Except that I know ahead of time that this upcoming year will be one of the most difficult I've ever had. The thing

I've avoided like the plague is becoming my life. My marriage is ending and we're making it official. In two days. Two measly, crummy, lets-pretend-they're-not-coming days.

Yeah, those two.

But here's the thing:

I'm realizing that the situations I most dread in life are always the ones that God uses. The most painful moments become the most beautiful in His story. I go into this knowing that. And dreading it still because I'm not Wonder Woman (despite my desperate attempt to find grown up Underoos). I'm just your average Christian girl whose life is apparently a train wreck (As it turns out, a lot of us are that way).

But I'm determined to do this: to not only learn from this time, but to grow, and think deeply, and consider every moment, so that when someone I care about has their own season of Not-Where-I-Want-to-Be I can help guide them through it.

Maybe you're that someone.

So, here we go. I'm pushing this battered old john boat away from the edge of safety . . . and heading straight for the shores of Not-Where-I-Want-to-Be.

The Small Beginnings

{Present Day}

Whether you're at the beginning of a New Year, or the beginning of a new week, if you are a single mom it may feel like every day is like stepping into new territory. Things that you once depended on to be steadies in your life are now gone. Regardless of if you feel you've handled it well up to this point, or you wish you'd done things differently, there is always time to choose a new path.

"Do not despise these small beginnings, for the Lord rejoices to see the work begin, to see the plumb line in Zerubbabel's hand."
Zechariah 4:10 (NLT)

I want to point us toward a better path. Even if it feels like it's not much of a start to you. The small beginnings often feel that way, don't they? They can take a tremendous amount of courage, and work, with little to no help or understanding from others. They can feel overwhelming and hopeless at times. Especially if those beginnings come at the end of something you once cherished. Even more so if it means a complete starting over in life.

If you are reading this book, you are likely at a crossroads. One that we're going to walk together. Not just you and me, but a whole team of single moms who have been there before us. Women from all walks of life, with a variety of stories as to how they became single moms, their personal struggles, and their triumphs. You see, I've been talking to them for years now. Many have reached out to me during struggles. Others have joined the private Facebook group and shared their stories and journey there. I've learned from them, and been amazed by them, and felt encouraged by them.

They're coming along side us, behind the scenes throughout this book, to encourage us, and empower us, and prove to us that we are not a small voice in the sea of voices. We are a much bigger voice than we ever imagined. In fact, with 15 million single moms in the US, there are nearly 2 single moms in every 10 moms you know. That's not one in a million—though it feels like it at times. Starting now, we're pulling these voices together.

So, envision yourself at this crossroads.

When I started my journey into single motherhood all I could envision was a dusty path in the middle of nowhere, facing a stop sign at a four way intersection. Occasionally a tumbleweed would blow by. Metaphorically, I was pretty sure that was my love life. Sometimes I'd sense a buzzard overhead, and possibly a rattlesnake—because I'm terrified of snakes, that's why. Regardless, my crossroad didn't appeal to me. All I wanted to do was get through it and move on to what I sensed was greener grass just ahead. Can you relate?

Behind us is the path we've taken up until now. Just up ahead (where we're fairly certain the green grass lives) is the path we've always envisioned ourselves on. It seems like such a happy place, just ahead. And did I mention, it's *just ahead*? And being on a straight path, obviously easy to get to.

On either side of us are the roads we must choose from instead.

I know, it seems unfair. Because we're wounded and should just be able to limp along the easy path, right? We're humiliated, we're angry. And we want nothing more than to plow through that stop sign we're facing and force our lives to take that path we've always envisioned. Not to mention that while we've been sitting here pondering our path, three of our friends have just passed through the stop sign as if it didn't exist and are now walking ahead of us — obviously heading to the happiest time of their lives.

We slump our shoulders and kick the dirt. Which doesn't help our cause any because it's so dusty on this path, it's hard to tell the dirt from the non-stop blowing of dust in our faces. Life seems blurred at the moment. The choice is not kind to us. Neither is the sun blaring down letting us know that time is moving on and we must choose.

We reach into our pocket to find a pair of perfectly good blinders we could wear. They're even pink and sparkly. With those on, we wouldn't have to acknowledge the paths to our left and right. We won't even see them anymore.

But we can't do that.

Seriously sister, don't do that.

Because believe it or not, we are exactly where God wants us. Not only that, but he's behind us, beside us, and even ahead of us on the turn in our path that we're getting ready to take. Not the one we planned on. The right hand turn we didn't expect. The one He knew about all along. And while all we may want to do is stand at that stop sign and lament what could have been, He is standing there to our right, offering His hand and ready to begin this journey with us—if only we'll allow it.

You see, there's something He knows that we don't. This single-mom life—this thing that terrifies us—is only a small part of our story. He knows what lies ahead and is hoping beyond all hope that we'll follow Him on the path He knows is best. Because at the end of that path is His best for us.

And, it's just ahead to the right.

This crossroads, this next path will determine the rest of our life—and the lives of our children. No pressure. I mean, our life has just been yanked out from under us, and we just need to get our feet under us so we can take control, right?

Um, no.

In fact, that's the last thing we want to do. In some way or another, doing just that has gotten us to this point in our lives. You know, the one we're now avoiding like the grey mush the lunch lady is trying to serve on parent's day at our children's school. We need to follow God's lead instead.

The way you choose to handle this next season in your life—and the lives of your children—will be a game changer. You are being given a unique opportunity—mid-life—to learn, and grow, and build something better for yourself. To look back on what's just happened, find your part in it, and choose something different. Something better.

His very best for you.

But it's going to take time. Some days you'll feel like simply getting your kids to school is all you can manage. And sweet friend, some days it will be. Still you'll push yourself to go on to work, to church, and all the other things in life you've built up to this point. You'll cling onto everything you had before for fear that it might be the one thing that keeps you from going under. Until the day that you realize some of those things are better let go. And your fingers will release, and you will soar a little inside at the thought of making a choice that is good.

> *What was your single greatest fear as a single mom?*
> "*Being alone. Even though I knew I could handle it alone, sometimes even having the illusion of someone there is comforting.*"
> -Melissa
> Single mom of 3

I have a feeling you've already made some choices that are good. Allow yourself to see that. Give yourself abundant grace during this time. To heal, instead of covering up your pain and pushing through life. If you're anything like me, you've likely been doing that for years in your last relationship. And, it's part of the reason why you're now on this path.

All you need to do is take the next step. Maybe for you, the tiniest step you can take is reading this book.

Don't despise the small beginnings. God doesn't.

Single Mom Challenge 1:

What are the things that exist on either side of that road for you? Do you have a well-intentioned friend who is trying to convince you to date before you're ready? An ex who is not being respectful at the moment?

One of the scariest things about being a single mom is the belief that we'll fail. But, like everything in life, things are often scarier in our minds than in real life. In fact, the truth about our fear is often the exact opposite of it.

So, we're going to steal fear's power by calling it out by name. By telling it we see it hiding there in the ditch, trying to trip us up. And, that we're not going there. Not giving in. And no longer afraid of it because we can see it clearly for what it is and the truth of what it isn't.

The biggest fears I have about being a single mom and the truths about those fears are:

1. Fear:

   _____

   Truth:

   _____

2. Fear:

   _____

   Truth:

   _____

3. Fear:

    _____

    Truth:

    _____

Laying the Plumb Line

It's hard starting over. For many of us, we never expected to, so there was no looking forward to a fresh start. Instead, it feels like a harsh slap in the face. But, we're here just the same. And, I'm determined we're going to make the best of it. Not just that, but we're going to make incredible strides that change our lives for the better.
And it all starts with a rebuilding of sorts.

If you've ever been on a construction site, the beginning can be fascinating. Before a builder lays the first brick for the foundation, they take the plan and carefully calculate their next step. If they are going to build a home that is 20 feet by 50 feet, they don't just "eye" it and hope they come close. They take careful measurements to ensure that the final building will be exactly what the plan calls for.

But, even the best laid plans can go awry. In fact, without the proper tools, a well-planned building can turn out to look more like a lean-to. So, how do they do it?

By laying out the lines ahead of time.

Taking the architectural plan, the builder follows it precisely, laying out an outline of the home using stakes to mark the corners of the foundation. This step is critical to ensure that the foundation is square. A poorly constructed foundation that is not accurately square will not only cause problems during construction, but could create a final building that is unstable.

So, they mark the four corners. Then they double check them. Laying mason lines that intersect at specific angles. Once those lines have been laid and the preliminary work complete, then—and only then—do they attach a plumb bob to each of the four intersections so that it will point to the exact foundation corners. The exact placement for the sturdiest possible build.

That's what this book is going to help you do. To build a new foundation for the life ahead of you. To show you the measurements you need to precisely consider as you're laying out the plan for your future as a single mom. To help you lay out the lines ahead of time. Because it's the work you do now, the hard work of planning and carefully measuring, that will allow you to lay the plumb with confidence. And ensure that your foundation is strong. It's a joy for God to see us finalize our exact plan with an action like this. Because it is then that He knows that a plan goes from being an idea in someone's head, to something more.

And it all starts with one step. A step that God rejoices in.

The Next Smallest Step

In my first days as a single mom, I was grasping to stay afloat. I looked everywhere for support and encouragement for single moms of faith—and found next to nothing. It felt like I'd just stepped into what I thought was a puddle, only to discover I was sinking below the surface.

And so I did what I'd been doing for the previous twelve years: I continued writing about my life and prayed that God would use me to encourage others, even when I felt I had nothing to give.

I was just . . . worn. You know?

My particular set of single mom problems built and built until I felt like the burden I carried would push me right under the water's surface. I began to ease off of the things that I needed most. Like going to church, and reading my Bible, and reaching out to others who would support me in love. My faith was at a standstill—even as I continued to write about it. I felt like I was becoming two different people: the one who encouraged others, and the one who barely held enough hope to get her own self through her situation.

You see, I'd come to realize a new truth through my ministry. As story after story of others just like me whose attempts to move on past their battered marriages were met with discouragement. With people who had no real

13

understanding. Who offered condemnation instead of hope. Who spoke of faith, while pointing out our lack. Of friends who'd chosen to step away. Of whispered rumors, and made up ones. Of emotional abuse and harassment: of sometimes them, and sometimes their children. A myriad of problems that no one would talk about, but most experienced. Alone.

It was the hidden norm. And the magnitude of it overwhelmed me.

And yet through it all, I kept telling myself that I'd chosen to step into these waters with Jesus. And because of that, even if I were to sit in a corner away from the world, in an attempt to hide from everyone including Him: He still wouldn't leave me there alone.

That I AM would fight for me.

It became my mantra, in fact.

And yet, I still just felt . . . worn.

I felt like I wasn't really even living most days. As if I was just on autopilot taking care of my kids and the basics we needed to get through. There was little joy, little hope, and little faith left in my God. I was starting to consider that my life would be infinitely easier if I just dropped all of this faith nonsense and started living like the rest of the world. They seem to handle divorce with ease. They seemed to bounce back quicker. They seemed happier sooner.

And I was so very very tired of being sad.

Then somehow, and for no apparent reason at all, with the tiny bit of strength I had left, I reached out to a godly group of women on Facebook that I barely knew. Telling them the truth of my situation. The truth I'd hidden because I didn't want to tell people my real story.

And a sweet friend replied:

"As I read your words, I'm imagining Jesus holding out his hand and saying, come with me. Just the next few steps. Just today. My yoke is easy."

And as I read her words, I wept. Because it spoke to my heart of hearts. The broken one. The battered one. The one that felt like life would never move forward despite everything I was doing to heal and help those around me to do the same. The one that wondered that if Jesus came to me and held out His hand, would I be too weak to take it now and follow.

Too . . . worn.

And I felt a spark ignite in my heart, sweet friends, as I realized another truth:

The reality is that all any of us has to offer Jesus is the same:

The next step.

Just today.

And accepting that and taking His yoke in place of our own is really the only way any of us has enough weight lifted off of our shoulders to be able to balance back on our own two feet so that we can step forward. Even the tiniest of steps. Even the smallest easing back into the waters with Him.

Even though we're worn.

Will you agree to do that with me? To come out of hiding? To give Him just today?

I pray you'll join me.

Single Mom Challenge 2:

We're going to change our lives for the better. That may mean starting over at day one, or simply lifting ourselves up to move in a better direction. It's going to feel risky. And daring. And you know what? It is. But, God rejoices to see that plumb line in your hand, sweet sister. To watch you lay the foundation of your new life.

And it starts right now.

The simple act of planning takes trust. And we're not doing this alone. We're going to trust God to show us what those next steps need to be. The best way to do that? Simply talking to Him through prayer.

Once you've done that, break your new start into three small action items that you need to take first in order to improve your situation, and give yourself a timeline to get each one done. These can be simple things such as spending 15 minutes doing something that makes you happy, to bigger issues like looking into a safer place for you and your children to live. But, they need to be real things that you know you need to do to make your life better. During your prayer time, ask God to make these action items clear. Deep down, we likely already know what these are.

Oh. And, see that check box? We're going to use it. In fact, it's going to make you feel so empowered by checking off the items on these challenges that you might just have

a stamp made with a big box that you can place all over
your house—just so you can check it off. Ready? You can
do this.

The first three action items I need to complete to
improve my situation are:

☐ _____

_____

_____

_____

Completed by _____

☐ _____

_____

_____

_____

Completed by _____

☐ _____

_____

_____

_____

Completed by _____

Chapter 2

First Steps

Change is inevitable. Growth is intentional.
– Glenda Cloud

If single parenthood has taught me anything in life, it's this: it is possible to live your life in 24-hour spurts.

In fact, in the beginning of my single mom status, it was literally all I could handle emotionally and physically. I prepped and was ready for the next day, and had no energy left to plan any further than that. If it didn't fall within the next 24-hour window, I gave it little thought. I couldn't let myself. Life was about survival. Moment to moment.

Sometimes that's a very good approach.

When life is overwhelming and you are unable to move forward, this is a good strategy to take. Remove everything from your plate that isn't absolutely necessary (appointments, obligations, expectations, plans, etc.) and only focus on what is the next most important task that will keep you and your children healthy and taken care of.

But you'll reach a point—someday—where it's time to move on from that.

This chapter is about taking steps. You know, those tiny little things your feet automatically do to move you and your life in a forward direction? They seem simple, right? I mean, you don't even think about them.

Unless you can't move forward.

But, the truth is, we are moving forward. Life is moving forward. With us, or without us. And while yes, there is a time for grieving our losses—and truly, one of the most important things we must do—there is also a time for stepping toward healing. Toward a version of our lives that we never saw coming. Toward the version that God knew about all along. Do you trust Him with that version?

This is a chapter with two lives.

For some of you, the grief process isn't complete. You aren't ready to move forward because it's too new. Too raw. You're too broken. Too shocked. But, sweet friend, we're going to move past that together. You're going to join the rest of us in this journey by faith and know that what we can do, you can do too. When we are at the end of this book, we're reaching back toward you because it will be your time to move. We're not leaving you behind in this. You have a new life to live.

For others of you, you've been at this a while but feel stuck somehow. You're able to move past some things but not others. Your heart longs to truly begin again, but your mind keeps pulling you back to look at your past. We're going to move past that together. We're linking arms on this journey and choosing a better path than the one the world encourages. We're leaving negative thinking behind us. We have a new life to live.

So let's get to it.

Refocusing

It took me a full two years before I was able to get a grip on my life after the end of my marriage. I was living moment to moment only able to focus on the immediate problem to be solved, the most critical tasks to be done. And I was beating myself up constantly about it. I felt so inept. So disjointed somehow. I didn't want to get out of bed anymore, much less make plans. I mean, I'd lost everything. My home. My dignity. My good name. My finances had been destroyed. My ex was relentlessly trying to place blame and make me pay for choosing to leave. Lifelong friends had faded away. Family members were blocking me on social media. People I'd never even spoken to in my town were having entire conversations about my life.

I was emotionally beaten down to the point of exhaustion.

I honestly didn't want to move on. I didn't want anything anymore. It didn't make sense to me to allow myself to want when clearly, your life could be taken from you in an instant—with no one left to care about what happened to you.

Except God.

In my mind, I had no one left but my children and God. And I lived in fear that my children would be the next to leave.

But can I tell you something? That's not such a terrible place to be. I know that sounds counterintuitive (aka crazy). But, think about this: when we are at that point, it's very easy to focus on what remains and start to rebuild. And if God and your children are all you have left, that's a solid foundation to start with.

Maybe you've heard about a guy named Job. Yeah, that guy in the Bible that no one wants to end up like, much less listen to. Reading about Job is like watching a bad movie on Netflix. You just want to get past it already, so you can binge on your next series (but you've already gone through all the episodes!). It's not a feel good story. It doesn't even actually end all that positively. But, it's real. It's one of the most realistic moments in the Bible. And we can learn a lot from that.

Job was a devout man who was blameless before God. So good in fact, that God used Job's obedience and faith to challenge the devil. The result? Essentially a living hell for Job. He loses everything from his wealth, to his children, to his good name, to his health. He hits rock bottom to no fault of his own. Essentially, Job suffers because he is among God's best, not His worst. But throughout his ordeal, though he is heartbroken and confused, suffering and destitute, he remains faithful to God. Even when he doesn't have the answers. Even when he questions God. Even when God doesn't answer him. He remains faithful, and God uses what happens in Job's life for generations to come.

But the fact remains that Job still had to suffer through it. The memory of his pain and suffering wasn't magically erased. The unsettling thoughts of how unfair it all was must have remained any time he looked back on that time in his life. He went through things we can't even imagine. But in the end, his suffering caused him to grow in his understanding of and his relationship with God.

When it was all said and done, in the end, he picked himself up and moved on. He had no choice. It's not that he suddenly felt better and got past it. He simply had no other choice. That's real life, friends. That's my life at the moment. And likely, it's yours too. It's time to move on. Even when we don't want to. Even when we don't see the point of it all--of anything at all. It's time to start fighting back. It's time to fight for our future.

If you allow it, there's room for a bigger picture in your life. There's room for more. And I want you to start expecting that. To expect more from your friends and family. More from your relationship with your children. More from life.

Because when we live moment-to-moment, we focus on the problems to be solved, the tasks to be done. And while there is a period in single motherhood when that is likely a necessary approach to take, we can't stay there forever. We need to remove those tent pegs and remember that there is more to life than the immediate. The frantic. The urgent.

We need to remember that God has a purpose for us that goes beyond just surviving.

But God Doesn't Have a Plan B

When I became a single mom, it wasn't a part of the plan. Life had taken an abrupt turn, and single motherhood (reluctantly) became my new reality.

I grieved in the beginning—and truth be told, for quite a while. Not only grieving for the losses that my children and I would suffer, but because this new life didn't match what I believed God was calling me toward in ministry. You see, I had a passion for the women in my church. I wanted to help them flourish in God's calling. I wanted to be known as a godly woman they could rely on. I wanted to serve God in the ministry He was so obviously laying on my heart: women's ministry.

I wasn't happy with God at the little turn off in my path—okay, it was a major swerve. The plan I had was moving along quite smoothly up to that point. I was the co-leader of women's ministry in my church. I was a writer for women's ministries across the nation. I was well on my way with Plan A when a boulder in the road forced me to instead choose Plan B.

In my anger, I went to church one Sunday, ready to talk to God about it. And when I say talk, I mean complain. Because let's face it, it just wasn't fair. You can imagine my surprise when a guest pastor stood up to talk about . . . our life plans. He looked me directly in the eye—really, he did—and said:

"God doesn't have a plan B for you. He has a plan A. And you're living it."

That was hard to swallow but undeniably meant for me. As I sat there I began to consider what that meant exactly. That He meant for my marriage to fall apart? That He didn't answer my years of praying to save it? That He planned for this pain in my children's lives?

I don't think for one second that's the case. But, I do believe this: regardless of the path we take in our lives, God is on it with us and can use every single bit of it for His glory. That He knows us so well, He knows the choices we will make and the reasons behind them—good or bad. And He is aware of the path we are about to walk long before we walk it. Kind of like any good parent and their child. Don't you know your child so well that you know the things they are likely to do? God knows us infinitely more so.

That means that in the midst of my pain, He not only knows about it, He is in it with me, and He feels it with me. Unlike me though, He knows what's to come next. How He will redeem this part of my life. And the beauty— yes beauty—that will someday result from it.

But in order to get to that beauty, I have to trust that God knows what He is doing through my pain. I have to trust that His plan is good.

God has a plan A for you, and you're living it.

Maybe this abrupt turn is something that you are struggling to accept. Maybe the vision you had of yourself is so far off course, you fear you're completely missing the point. Maybe you're in a period of suffering that doesn't make sense to you at all. Maybe your heart is so broken you feel that you'll never be happy again. Maybe you simply feel like a wanderer.

That, sweet friend, is not part of God's plan.

But it is the exact plan of the enemy.

o The enemy whispers that what you're going through is not right. Not fair. Not the plan at all.

o The enemy whispers that God has forgotten you. That your place in God's plan doesn't make a difference.

o The enemy wants nothing more than to make you believe that what God has planned for you at this point in your life is not enough.

o The enemy wants you to believe that this season of single motherhood can't be used for God's glory.

But it's a lie.

Where you are right now—the town you live in, the home you live in, the people that remain in your life, the new ones He brings in, the suffering you endure, the miniscule hope you hold onto—is precisely where God knew you would be. It's a difficult part in His larger plan for your life. It's not where He'll always have you. But it's exactly where you are supposed to be in this moment. Do you trust Him with that?

Rest assured, whatever change your plans have taken, you haven't missed your calling. You haven't somehow walked past the love of your life on the street and not noticed. You haven't misunderstood where He wants you, or the people He is calling you to minister to. You haven't ruined anything at all.

The beautiful surprise about difficult times in our faith is that when our plans don't work the way we thought or planned them to be, it's often because God's plan for us is more than what we were allowing in our lives. He's not surprised at the turn of events, of what has come your way, or even how you've reacted to it.

It's plan A, after all, and you're doing just fine.

So start viewing your situation in a new light. Today. Join God where you are right now. Right this moment. Even if you can't thank Him for it, or understand it, or really even accept it. Know that He is with you on this path, just one small step ahead.

Take the step to join Him there. He's waiting.

Getting in on God's Game Plan

Think about this: When we aren't intentional, we waste.

This is true in our refrigerator. This is true with our gas tank. This is true with our money. This is true with our career. This is true with our relationships. We have to be intentional, or we risk wasting.

This summer was one of the first in years that I completely forgot to do a summer bucket list with my kids. Never done one? They're awesome. At the end of each school year, we take out a piece of paper and make a list of all of the great summer activities we want to experience. It gets us excited about the new season ahead, allows us to dream a little, and (mostly) keeps me from letting time slip away while I'm working like crazy to hold things together. I like to be intentional with our summer because I know it's important to not only take care of my kids but to build memories with them. Essentially, it's there to keep us from missing out.

But, because I wasn't as intentional as I'd been in years past, the summer flew by us with barely anything done. No trips to the beach. No visits to museums or zoos we'd been longing to go to. No big slumber parties with friends to celebrate our new freedom. We missed out, because I was still lingering moment to moment and forgot to look forward.

Are you there with me?

When we aren't intentional, we risk the hunkering down that pain can cause as we hide to protect ourselves.

And if we stay in that mode too long, we will forget that we are also in a season with our children that won't last forever. We'll come out of our shells of protection just as our daughters are walking across that stage to accept their diplomas, or as our sons are looking at their first car, and realize that we allowed precious years to go by where we didn't shake ourselves out of our rut and get back to life.

So shake it off.

Seriously, there's a theme song and everything for this moment. Truly, truly, if Taylor Swift hadn't written our theme song, a single mom would have.

I don't say this lightly, sweet friend. I know the pain you've suffered. I know the humiliation. The anger. The sadness. The loneliness. The bitterness. The anxiety. The fear. I know it all because I'm living it. But, we can't let it hold us down. I'm not saying this will get rid of the pain. I'm simply saying we're not going to let it attach to every single part of our lives. We have to shake off the hold pain has. Shake off the pain of what's happened to you, the pain of your loss—maybe even the pain you've caused—so that we can reach back into life.

Because we not only get one chance at life, but one chance at being a mom with our children in our homes. Let's fill those homes with laughter, and joy, and the example that life can be hard, but God is bigger and will help us to overcome. Let's number our days well, so that we capture the bigger picture of what God is calling us toward.

<u>Single Mom Challenge 3:</u>

If we are going to get in on God's game plan we have to make an effort to see beyond ourselves and our situation to discover what He's doing. The only reason we think He's not there, is because we aren't focusing on noticing all the ways He actually is. He's never left us alone for one solitary second.

And starting now, we're going to watch Him, and take notes in a journal. Your first assignment?

Buy a journal (mine will likely be pink) and some fun pens. Seriously. Buy some fun pens. They make everything better. You don't have to spend a lot of money. In fact, I'm going to the Dollar Tree in a few hours to buy mine.

This is your tool to freedom. This won't be some random journal that we are going to hold onto for twenty years and write in every six months. This is our ticket out of the muck. The most crucial thing we need in our plan with God.

He's moving. And we're going to record Him.

Now obviously, I'm a writer. But I'm not a journaler. The main reason? I have terrible handwriting. I mean terrible. I'm the type of person who makes a quick list before I go to the store, then get there, and can't read it. It's kind of sad considering my career is in design where I basically draw for a living. You'd think I could at least write, right? Ahem. But, I'm committing to this alongside you. I'm kind of excited about seeing the unexpected places He takes me, the things He shows me that I was too busy to see before, and the ways He's going to use it to heal my heart.

So let's do this thing!

We're going to work through some challenges in this book that will be a part of your journal. But, I also want you to use it however you see fit. Pray in it. Make notes in it. Write down encouraging quotes in it.

Just. Use. It.

But only for good. The goal is healing. So, if you have a breakdown and write it all out in your journal—and every sentence is about how much you hate life at the moment— go back and look at it later to see how far you've come. We're not going to ignore the hard things. The hard times. But we're going to make it a goal to push toward healing.

Agreed?

At the end of this book, you'll find that you've healed a little, grown a little, and will start to realize that there is more out there that you want in life. You'll expect more from your future than you allowed in your past.

More fun in your family time.

More adventure.

More love.

And you'll have it in writing, friend. Hopefully in bright colors. So, again, buy the fun pens. Just do it. Then meet me in the next chapter.

Chapter 3

Clinging to the Rock

During my first month of Not-Where-I-Want-to-Be, I hunkered down. Not necessarily on purpose, but maybe unconsciously so. I knew there were limited things that I could handle with my emotions pouring out at random moments and so I withdrew.

Everyone told me it was the worst possible thing I could do. That I needed people. That I should reach out to others. But, I felt like God was saying otherwise. I needed to grieve. I needed to sleep. I needed to heal.

That month was a covering of sorts. A bandage over the wound that felt so deep I thought I'd be scarred for life. So deep and raw in the beginning that I knew I couldn't handle an offhanded comment, or pity, or anything beyond a simple "hello." Truth be told, even that was too much at times.

Unless interaction was a necessity such as taking my kids to school, or going to the grocery store, or limping into church, I didn't do it. I had a limited amount of "smile-time" and just underneath the surface I knew was a crushed heart ready to pour out at any moment. I even cancelled a major work event that I was required to be at for my job (praise God for my amazing boss) because I knew that there was no way I could sit in a meeting for eight hours straight and not have a crying meltdown at some point.

I pulled away in pain, so that I could catch my breath again.

And while that might not be the recommended way to handle such a situation, it gave me an unexpected gift. Without all the normal chatter in my life, I was struck by the quiet. And in that clear quiet, I was suddenly open to talk to God more.

In those moments when I was heaving uncontrollably and seriously understood how a person could literally die of a broken heart, He was with me. And it wasn't a pat thought in my head like "yes, good Christian girl, God is with you." I mean He was *with* me. In a house that was completely empty and filling with my sobs, I could tell that someone else was there too.

And so I began an ongoing conversation. One that still isn't over, and I pray never will be. When I had the urge to talk to a girlfriend but couldn't stand the thought of opening that wound to explain all the dirty details of what I was going through, I talked to God, who had witnessed it firsthand. When I longed for companionship so deeply it felt paralyzing, He held me. When I felt betrayed, and angry, and hopeless, I asked Him to make his presence known to me in real and tangible ways.

And you know what? He never let me down. Not once. And I learned that something I'd always heard about Him was true: no matter what you're going through, He will *never* leave you in it. No matter how badly you've been hurt, no matter how ugly you feel, no matter how much you doubt that you can trust anyone, He understands because he sees you.

Just like he saw another single mom in the Bible.

The God Who Sees

Hagar was an Egyptian handmaid of a barren wife named Sarai (Sarah), who gave her to Abram (Abraham) as a second wife so that he could bear a child. Now, while we may or may not agree with the premise behind this, it's clear that Hagar entered into this relationship honestly. When Hagar became pregnant, she began to feel differently about her mistress, Sarai, and began to treat her poorly. We can all imagine that there was likely jealousy involved. And Sarai, heartbroken over the fact that she could not provide a child for her husband, began to grieve this situation.

When Abram discovered Sarai's grief, he allowed her to deal with Hagar however she felt necessary. Her treatment of Hagar was so harsh, Hagar fled for her life. But, along the way of her escape, an angel appeared to her. Not only to take care of her, but to encourage her to return to Sarai and Abram, to have the baby that God would use to build a nation. God reached out to her in her loneliness—*before* she reached out to Him—and gave her the promise of a future. From that day forward, Hagar used another name when she referred to God. She said, "You are the God who sees me."

Years later, when her child, Ishmael, was a teenager, sparks of jealousy began to fly between Sarai and Hagar again. Sarai had been gifted with her own child, and it would seem that the jealousy between the two children existed as well. This time, Sarai was once again allowed to handle the situation as she saw fit. And, she saw fit to banish Hagar and her son to the wilderness.

Girl. I mean, really.

There have been times when I've read this story and thought that Hagar deserved what happened to her. I mean, she was sleeping with another woman's husband for goodness sake. Even though at that time in history, having multiple wives was acceptable. But, as I read this story as a single mom, I began to understand Hagar's side.

She went into a relationship honestly and openly. She raised her child with his father, even though she knew that he loved another. And even when she was banished, she willingly obliged and left everything she'd known for years.

I imagine that I'd have thrown what's known as a hissy fit in the South. That I'd have been mouthy, and demanding, and probably insisted that my son was the rightful heir as the firstborn and that I deserved to be an equal to Sarai. I also have to wonder if deep inside Hagar felt contempt toward her masters who were Jewish. She was an Egyptian. The same race who lorded over the Jewish nation only a few generations before.

By all accounts, Hagar was treated unfairly. Though she followed through with what she was asked, she was abandoned by everyone she trusted. Can't you just see the other women coming out of their tents as Hagar left town, whispering and possibly smiling over her misery? Maybe some looked at her as a mistress. Even Abram, though worried about his son, didn't stand up for Hagar and let Sarai have her way. I've always found it interesting that Abram wasn't called into account about the safety of his wife and child. Until I realized that she was leaving what was considered a marriage, and that is how many women are treated as they leave theirs, regardless of the circumstances.

Can you relate?

Alone, abandoned, and destitute, Hagar and her child wandered into the wilderness with nothing but the bread and water Abram gave as she left. Bread and water, people. The bare minimum that would probably be acceptable to society.

Thrust into single motherhood, forced to leave her home, and facing an uncertain future, it was her son's cries that God responded to. A God that wasn't typically worshipped by Egyptians. A God they had come to know through Abram. God not only saved them from their immediate situation, but "God was with the boy as he grew up in the wilderness."

I love that. While the mother was so broken she could only accept that their fate was death, God heard the cries of her son, and stepped in to take care of them **both**. A God they came to worship because of the marriage she was in. A God she may not have known otherwise.

He'll do the same for you and your children.

Maybe you need to restore your relationship with God. Return to Him. This is your chance. Maybe your one opportunity in life, to begin anew. To focus your efforts on growing deeply in the Lord.

Ultimately, more than anything, God desires a closer relationship with you. He longs for you to turn toward Him and find comfort in His presence. That relationship is a priceless gift that not everyone experiences. And that's not the only gift he's hoping you'll ask Him for.

<u>Single Mom Challenge 4:</u>

Growing your relationship with God starts with you. He is waiting and will rush to join you. Will you grow it by starting a One-Year Bible? By joining or beginning a Bible Study? By making time each day to spend with Him in prayer? Growing this relationship may feel uncomfortable in the beginning, but it will eventually become one of the most natural things in your life. If you don't know where to start, begin with a conversation with God (another word for prayer). Don't wait another minute.

The first three things I will do to grow my relationship with God are:

1. _____

_____

_____

2. _____

_____

_____

3. _____

_____

_____

Transfer these to your journal.

Three things I feel that God "sees" that no one else does:

1. _____

   _____

   _____

2. _____

   _____

   _____

3. _____

   _____

   _____

Transfer these things to your journal.

The Gift That Reveals His Heart for You

When I was ready to get back to life—and by that I mean speak to others in public without having to run into the bathroom and cry—I sat down with a godly girlfriend and asked her advice about the path I was on. Up until this time, I'd never had a lengthy conversation with this friend. We were in some church groups together, and I knew that she'd been a single mom when she was younger. I felt like God was leading me to her, and I willingly obliged. What she told me was life changing. And, honestly, changed the path I would have chosen.

As we sat over salads at Panera, I geared that conversation for an hour toward everything I could think of that didn't have to do with my situation. It was kind of like knowing you need to remove a Band-Aid, but you're afraid of the pain of pulling it off. I wanted to talk to her. I felt like God was pushing me to talk to her. But, I was so afraid of what she might say because deep down, I knew it was something God wanted me to hear. I mean, I was leaving my marriage. I was a godly woman who had been a leader in my church women's group. In the back of my mind I had a fear that I was about to be reprimanded instead of encouraged (can you say: the enemy at work?). Afterward I felt foolish for even thinking that way.

THE SINGLE MOM CHALLENGE

In one of the most loving but firm conversations I've ever experienced, she made things clear to me that I want to make clear to you. Her advice was essentially this:

First, whatever it is that you're going through, God's already there. He's behind it, he's in it, and he's ahead of it. There's nothing in this in which you are alone. Nothing. Because unlike the rest of us, God is an eye witness in your life. He understands your situation better than anyone.

Second, as you go into this new part of your life, you need to be careful that you don't let your focus sway. Because people are going to talk. Lies are going to be told. And some will share your story whether you talked to them about it or not. Some of it will hurt you. Just don't let any of it distract you.

Third, (Remember that crossroads we talked about earlier?) as you step out onto this path, you need to know that there are ditches that dip down and then level back out to the ground on either side. God is on that road with you. But, on either side, across the ditch, are the distractions. They may come as a friend who wants to push you faster than you're able or willing to go, or a dating website you don't need to get involved with at the moment. They may come as the person who hurt you and put you in this place, or your well-meaning parent who has a knack for making you feel reprimanded.

Listen to me here: **Stay out of that ditch.**

Don't allow yourself one step in either direction no matter how much you think it might be okay to just visit. Focus your whole self, your whole heart, on God and the new path He is leading you on right now. You can't handle more than that. You can't. So don't fool yourself.

Can you say incredibly wise? I rushed home and wrote down everything I could remember so that I would never forget. It felt like God had spoken directly to me through my friend.

It was during this meeting that she recommended something else that I would eventually cling to in the months to come: finding a life verse for this season of my life. It has been the single most powerful part of my healing through this process, and I want you to find one as well. Maybe this will be the first one you've ever asked for. I'd actually done it before, but not quite so directly.

I never understood the power of a life verse until I prayed about finding one for the first time. I was a new Christian at the age of 30 and had a pretty messy wake behind me. I felt alone, unloved, and was certain that I was cursed to be that way my entire life. I couldn't trust anyone—but Him, and struggled emotionally to connect through anything other than a surface relationship with other women.

I'm not sure where I first heard about life verses, but I shyly prayed for one. Honestly, I didn't think God would hear me. I thought it would be another prayer to bounce off the walls of heaven and come back with deafening silence. Boy was I wrong. Watch out when you do this, because it might just blow you out of the water.

He gave me:

"I will repay you for the years the locusts have eaten."
Joel 2:25 (NIV)

I cannot tell you how powerful this verse was to a girl who'd felt abandoned, who'd been disowned, and at the age of 30 could honestly say she wasn't sure there was a single person in her life beyond her children who loved her. She was broken, and convinced she would always be so.

With that verse, came both a promise and a vision. A promise that God would restore the lost years, and a vision that what had been taken would someday be rebuilt. Looking back on my life at that point, it appeared that locusts had come through and stripped everything bare. It's what they're best known for.

In fact, in Biblical times, an invasion of locusts was one of the worst things that could happen to a country. Though they were incredibly sturdy and could jump nearly 200 times their own height, they had no control

47

over where they went. They were simply carried where the wind blew. Because of that, they often appeared as great masses raining down on any one area. These "darkeners of the sun" advanced slowly and were relentless until they destroyed every green thing in their path, leaving a wasteland behind.

In many ways, they were controlled by God. Where the wind blew, they destroyed. And yet, he could choose to heal a land—or a person's life—in that same controlled way.

At my lowest level in Not-Where-I-Want-to-Be, my sweet friend reminded me of how powerful life verses could be, so I asked for another.

He gave me:

God is within her; She will not fall;
Psalm 46:5 (NIV)

I literally cried at the sight of it. I immediately made it the cover photo on my phone and couldn't stop reading it over and over again. It was a much needed reminder to me that God was not only with me, but within me. And though the road I'm walking with Him is surely going to be tough, I will not fall. He won't let me.

So, how did I know these were my life verses?

1. I prayed for them. God assures us that when we ask for things in His name, He will give them. And

since He communicates through His word, and He wants nothing more than to be in a mutually involved relationship with us, He loves it when we take the first step toward Him.

2. I was immediately "struck" when I read the verse. You know that thing they do in the movies where something is revealed to the main character and the camera slowly moves toward them as they realize a truth and the rest of the background fades? It seriously was kind of like that. It caught my breath in a way, and then I wondered if this was "the one" He meant for me. The second one brought me to tears (another good indicator).

3. You can't stop thinking about the verse. In both cases, I asked God for the verse, was "struck" with the verse, then couldn't stop thinking about it. When I asked God if that was the one, He just kept bringing it to mind.

4. They rang true to what my heart needed to hear the most at the time. God is not small time. He's not going to give you something that makes you go, "Meh." He's going to drop a verse on you that makes you go, "Really? I mean seriously, that's mine?" It will be something you've longed to hear. Something you need desperately at the time. Something that makes you feel known.

If there is ever a time in your life that you need to feel like someone you trust knows you, it's now. Don't delay this part of the process. Go find His verse for you.

Single Mom Challenge 5:

Discovering your life verse for this season can be affirming, uplifting, and empowering. God knows what it is that you need to hear the most in order to be encouraged. He wants to remind you of all that He sees in you and all that He has planned for your life. This may be one of the most important prayers you've ever prayed.

Pray as you feel led. But, if you are struggling to find the words, know that He hears you still. Simply come to Him with the intention of finding your life verse for this season in your life. Then, watch carefully in the coming days for His confirmation.

Once you have a verse or verses, write it here. Then, add the confirmations you discover.

My life verse for this season:

_____

_____

_____

_____

_____

_____

_____

Confirmations of my life verse:

_____

_____

_____

_____

_____

_____

_____

_____

_____

_____

_____

Transfer these things to your journal.

The Keeper of Your Heart

There is nothing more important to your success as a single mom, than your relationship with God. The more time you spend building that relationship, the more you lean into Him, the fewer problems you will experience outside of it.

But, I know what you're thinking: WHEN do you have time? And, I hear you. There is nothing more stressful to single moms than the lack of time they have available to do—well, anything. And, I'm painfully aware that for many, the church can be a painful place. And while I believe in community, and the local church, and know that healing can come through these, I also understand the inclination to shy away. To protect. Both your heart, and your children's. That's why we're focusing on relationship here.

Your personal relationship with God.

And while that might be daunting—don't let it deter you. Just as you long to have a loving relationship with your children, God longs for the same with you. All He sees is his precious little girl, and longs to know you better now that you're grown. Sweet friend, let Him. It will be the single most important thing you ever do. He changes lives. And, He's ready to change yours. Not based on how often you go to church, or how many Bible verses you know (although I pray those things will become part of your life). He's more interested in your heart, and you getting to know His.

So, how does a single mom with zippo time on her hands grow this relationship?

- o Simply talk to Him. It really is that easy. In your everyday voice, in the conversational style you use with everyone else, talk to Him. If it's ten seconds or ten minutes. You've never met a better listener.
- o Pray over your children. If you're not a prayer, this can feel awkward at first. But, there is nothing that brings two parent's hearts together more than discussing their children's future. Never forget, they are yours and His.
- o Sit before Him in total silence. Not a talker? Don't know what to say? Sweet girl, He already knows. Simply sit in silence dedicated to Him.
- o Sing to Him. Find a song that speaks to your heart and sing it out to Him.
- o Journal or draw. Again, it's not about what you say. Doodle if you want to.
- o Read a one-year Bible. In about fifteen minutes a day, you'll push through in a year. Don't have that much time? Read it in two. (Yeah, we're rule-breakers here.)

The point is that He is anxiously waiting to join you wherever you are. He's not concerned with when or where, how or how long. He is the vine, girls. We are the branches. The closer we stay to the vine, the more nutrients we receive, and therefore, the better pieces of fruit. The further away we move from the vine and its life-giving nutrients, the more likely we are to be pruned as we leave ourselves dangling for others to grab.

I can't stress enough how vital this relationship is to you and your children. This relationship has to become a priority for you in this season of your life so that when you are tempted—and you will be—to move on to your next romantic relationship with the wrong person, or to take risks that you shouldn't, or to listen to advice that is unwise, you'll have the strength to realize that is not where God is leading you. Don't allow yourself to step off the path, over those ditches, and visit the parallel paths you may see others on.

He sees you in the wilderness and is ready and waiting to lead you out of it.

Get Back to Church

I started slinking into church. Avoiding.

The same church that I'd served in children's and women's ministry for years. The same church I'd attended Bible studies, and Bible classes. In a moment's notice, my world had changed and I was filled with dread about how the people of my church would react. I knew what they thought about divorce. I'd heard the sermons. The comments. The suggestions about others who had gone before me.

I cried through those first services and wondered what people thought, even though most members I'd reached out to were completely supportive of my circumstances. Still, it seemed that eyes were always on me. So much so, that I found it difficult to concentrate on what I needed most at the moment: time with God.

For the first time in my life I thought about the single moms that came before me. I'd seen them slink in, avoiding. And I wondered if I'd been kind or judgmental.

The truth is that single moms leave the church in droves. In droves. According to Jennifer Maggio, founder of *The Life of a Single Mom Ministries*, some studies suggest as many as 67% of single moms currently do not attend church – many citing fear of being judged as key. And while some will say that the church is not to be condemned when we are hurt by those in it and feel the need to leave, it still matters.

It matters.

THE SINGLE MOM CHALLENGE

Because not only is that mom leaving at a crucial time in her life, she is taking an average of 2 children with her. Children who have also suffered a devastating loss. Children who need to know about a Savior who hasn't left them alone in this great sadness they are feeling over the change in their family.

If you've left the church as a single mom, or even changed churches, there is no condemnation. In fact, I'll bet that in your specific circumstances, you should have left.

> **How did your faith play a role during this time in your life?**
> "*It was a difficult but sweet time for me in my faith in the Lord. I was terrified of stepping out on my own. I moved to a small town the name of which means something like "the edge of the rock" and I sort of laughed like it was this little joke between me and God – here I was, moving to a place where I would be seated on the Rock – depending on Him to meet my needs and comfort me*"
> -Caroline, single mom of 1, recently remarried

Maybe leaving was the only way to keep your faith intact. To be able to leave the door open to returning someday.

God knows. He sees. He is more brokenhearted than anyone at the way you've suffered. At the way others have reacted. At the words said that have broken both of your hearts. He's been sitting with you as you moved slowly to the back of the church, until one day, you simply stopped coming in at all.

Maybe your someday is now.

He longs for you to return. And not to the back pew.

He's inviting you to the front. Where the focus is on Him. Where the looks fall behind you, and you no longer care about them. Back to worshiping Him. And fellowshipping with Him. And looking to Him to remind you of just how valuable you are to His church.

To bring back not only His daughter, but your sons and daughters as well. Because a time will come in your children's lives that rock them to the core. They will be hurt by something or someone in the church. It's almost as if it's a part of the Christian walk, isn't it? And in that moment, they need to remember a mother who put the pain aside, and chose to focus on her Savior instead. Who forgave, and forgot, so that she could move forward in Him.

This Sunday, you'll find me in a pew, with my children beside me. I hope you'll join me there.

__Single Mom Challenge 6:__

I know you don't want to. Really. I've been there. But, some things are for your own good (like that broccoli you make your kids eat) and you know I'm right. This week, I want you to go to church. Any church. Anywhere. Even online.

If you no longer have a church, spend time on Sunday looking into churches in your community. Reach out to someone you know that has a strong faith and find out where they attend.

Next Sunday's Date:_____

Church I attended:_____

Or

Churches I researched:

_____

_____

_____

_____

_____

Transfer these to your journal

Chapter 4

Addressing the Wound

Before we can fully move on from our past, we need to face it head on.

This chapter is going to be hard for all of us. But I promise you two things: 1. This chapter is necessary to our moving forward, and 2. You will be glad that you walked through it when we get to the end.

Gathering Courage

I'm basically a scaredy cat. Except that I have a really good game face.

I make all kinds of plans to do things that scare me for the simple fact that hunkering down and hiding isn't always good for me. Last fall, I made a plan that terrified me. A friend whom I love and admire deeply had just written a book and was holding a retreat across country to launch it. This wasn't going to be your average book launch. She was ministering to the women who had chosen to come alongside her in her ministry. This amazing woman had gathered seventy or so other amazing, godly women and we were going to be getting knee deep with Jesus over the weekend.

It was something I needed desperately and I knew it. But after the prior two years, I no longer trusted people. I no longer wanted friends. I no longer liked to be around other women. Maybe—like me—community was what hurt you the deepest. Their comments, and looks, and disqualifying of your friendship rocked you to your core.

I was seriously a wreck over it.

The closer the retreat drew, the more reasons I came up with as to why I should just cancel. My friend would be crazy busy and probably wouldn't even notice if I wasn't there. I'd just gone through the roughest two years of my life and I couldn't take one more difficult encounter. Only recently had I even begun to come back out of hiding to participate in my community. It was hard to be around any people at all because of the way I'd been treated when my marriage fell apart. I'd become a recluse of sorts, and quite honestly, I liked it that way.

But, just as I'd pushed myself out into the world again, I had an aching feeling (and by aching I mean painful and nauseous) that God wanted me to put myself into this very large group of Christian women and ease into getting to know them. Honestly, I don't like these kinds of things. At. All. I didn't even know how to make friends anymore.

But I forced myself to buy a plane ticket to a state I'd never been, with money I couldn't really afford to spend, and set up rides with people I'd never met to get to the retreat center.

Then something I didn't expect happened.

From the moment I stepped off the plane, every woman I encountered seemed to be the most loving, accepting, and gracious woman I'd ever met. Then, I met another. And another. I heard others comment more than once at the retreat about how unbelievably kind and considerate this group of women were. It was as if God hand-picked these women to surround this hardened and battered heart at a time when I wasn't willing to expose it to another soul. If I hadn't understood that it was God, I would've felt duped somehow.

It caused me to talk to people I never would have talked to before. And add to conversations I would have shied away from a week before. And even—to share my story when I couldn't stand to hear myself telling it even one more time.

I told these women more about what was going on with me than I'd told anyone—ever. I sat around the lunch table and began answering a question someone asked me. Quite honestly, the fact that someone even noticed me long enough to ask me a question shocked me—I'd just felt invisible for so long. And before I knew it, I'd spilled the beans. The ugly, sticky, what I felt like were disgusting beans that had become my life.

I remember being mid-story when I realized what I'd just unknowingly done: poured out my heart to a group of women. I think I must have choked out the last few words as I prepared for what I knew was coming: the reprimand.

Because in the previous two years, there wasn't a single time that I shared even the tiniest parts of my life in Christian circles without one person rising to the surface who felt the need to make it clear that they couldn't accept what I'd done by getting a divorce. Without even asking the whys behind it. And in my mind, implying that God wouldn't accept it either.

My face was so flushed, I could feel it burning. I literally held onto my chair. And then, one woman began to speak. As she did, the others around the table leaned in closer nodding in agreement. Someone took my hand. Another touched my shoulder. They gathered around me, listening—even crying—as they asked questions that dove deeper into my grief. They asked about my children. They asked if I had a support system. I could see the genuine love and concern in their eyes—without a single hint of anything else.

Then, they thanked me. Thanked. Me. For giving them insight into what a single mom goes through.

I could hardly believe what was happening.

At the end, they offered to pray for me. To pray for the same girl who'd sat in church begging God to send godly women into her life, with none surfacing that would stick around the mess I was walking through.

It was one of the most healing experiences in my walk as a single mom. And I know without a doubt that God wanted it for me. He wanted to show me that His church, while not perfect, is still full of people who love as He's asked them to. With people who are able to look beyond the biases some hold, and see the person behind it. With people who genuinely want to help those whom God has brought before them.

I've often wondered if they had any idea of the kicking and screaming it took me to get there. The moments I just wanted to slip into my covers during the weekend and hide from all of them. The many ways I looked for every excuse under the sun not to accept this opportunity.

I want you to take a chance like that with this chapter. I hope you will begin to reexamine the things that have hurt you in the past so that you can move forward into the future God has planned for you. He can't move without you alongside Him. And He can't move until you're ready.

> **What is one thing you would warn single moms not to do?**
>
> *Don't think you can do this on your own steam/resources - seek help from friends in church, neighbors, family and seek counseling if you feel the slightest bit overwhelmed. You may look fine on the outside, but inside your world is falling around your feet. You need help rebuilding.*
>
> Wendy, single mom of 1

This is your moment to choose to do something you fear, while relying on God to heal you through it.

Examining the Wound

Since starting *The Christian Single Mom* ministry, I've talked with lots of single moms from all walks of life. Some have been helped tremendously by their church family.

Others have felt isolated to the point of leaving the church they once loved. Some have had family rally around them. Others have had family isolate them. I've heard stories of absolute abandonment. And I've heard stories of people who stepped in to change what could have been a devastating situation for a mom and her children.

Everyone's experience is different. Maybe you had a church that supported you through thick and thin. Maybe you faced biases in your church. Maybe you had some family members that rose to the surface to support and love you. Maybe you had an encounter with someone that left you emotionally devastated. There are as many experiences as there are single moms.

But, there are also similarities between us.

As I started to delve deeper into this issue, I wanted to get a better understanding from other single moms out there. I didn't want this story to just be my story—I wanted it to be ours. I wanted to know who they felt hurt them the most. Were they upset with specific people? Their family? Their children? Did they blame God for what happened to them?

So, I reached out to other single moms on my social media pages and asked them this one question, and I want you to answer it too:

In your journey as a single mom, please rank these people or categories of people in order of who you feel caused you the most emotional harm whether intentional or not. The number 1 would indicate the least amount of harm. The number 9 would indicate the most amount of harm.

— Friends
— Church Members
— People in My Community
— Christians I encountered in person or online
— Church Leaders
— Family
— Former Spouse or Partner
— My Children
— God

From the nine categories that were given, it probably doesn't surprise you that Former Spouse or Partner was the most commonly listed category that caused the most harm. In fact, 85% of single moms surveyed chose this category. This, we can all understand, right? This we've witnessed or experienced firsthand. This, we likely saw coming.

But the next two categories surprised even me. Honestly, I thought that friends and family—maybe even community—would be the next in line. I've had so many women reach out to me about these very relationships and how they hurt them in the process of their marriages falling apart instead of rallying around them like they expected. But it was the church and its members and leadership that had hurt them the most.

2. Church Members
3. Church Leaders

So the top three causes of emotional harm in our lives were from the two places that we cherish most as Christians: our homes and our church family.

Just looking at the numbers made me both saddened and angry. Several women who responded to the survey told me the same. It's hard to think that a place that you would trust with your heart, mind, and soul would be the place that caused more pain on top of your already broken heart. But, it's common. It's not in your head. You haven't imagined it. Or made something out of nothing.

It's also common that our faith slips while we are going through this.

And we're not going to let that happen. Not even one more millimeter. Because our God is a Redeemer, sweet friend. And He's going to redeem our story starting today.

Pushback When You Point Out the Church

Before I gave that survey, I had my own experiences to back up the study. And I want you to know that I truly hoped that my situation wasn't as common as I expected it to be. I wanted others to have walked a different path. I hoped that it was all in my head to be quite honest. Because I know that calling out the church on an issue — any issue — is painful for anyone who loves their church as much as I did. As much as the other women I've spoken to.

I've heard from the other side of the question too. I've had uncomfortable conversations where those people warned me about blaming the church for my pain, or for pointing out problems with the way the church handles single moms. I had one person angrily suggest that they were tired of everyone blaming the church for every issue under the sun and that you couldn't blame the church for a situation your choices created.

I understand their concerns. I do. But I also wonder if they've ever experienced the kind of wounds I'd experienced or the ones that had been brought to my attention by other single moms. Yes, the church is not there to meet my needs, it's there to encourage my relationship with God. But, there are times when they do harm to that relationship whether they mean to or not.

And not discussing those issues does nothing more than place the blame back on the person who was hurt.

I had to look at the overall picture, remove the "church" from my concerns and instead consider how God would look at those wounds. Would it matter to Him that women were leaving the church at this crucial time in their lives? Faithful, dedicated, godly women who were falling by the wayside at the time when they needed others the most? Would it matter to Him that people calling themselves Christians were shaming women into staying in abusive relationships in order to salvage their family as if the actual people within the family were less important than the whole? Would it matter to Him that church members felt the need to point out divorce as the "unforgiveable" sin while supporting the substance abusers, adulterers, and other deviant behaviors that were the core problem of these family break-ups? Would it matter to Him that these women felt abandoned by Him because of the way they felt abandoned by the church?

Yes.

It matters to Him. *You* matter to Him.

In the parable of the lost sheep in Luke 15, Jesus told this story:

"Suppose one of you has a hundred sheep and loses one of them. Doesn't he leave the ninety-nine in the open country and go after the lost sheep until he finds it? And when he finds it, he joyfully puts it

on his shoulders and goes home. Then he calls his friends and
neighbors together and says, 'Rejoice with me; I have found my lost
sheep.' I tell you that in the same way there will be more rejoicing in
heaven over one sinner who repents than over ninety-nine righteous
persons who do not need to repent."(NIV)

The shepherd (Jesus) was willing to leave all of the others behind in order to save the one. That one is you, sweet friend, and He'd put them all behind Him if that's what it took to save you.

To. Save. You.

Resetting Our Minds

My experience with the church fell somewhere in the middle. Some in the church rallied around to help me once I shared what was truly going on in my marriage. Others tried to shame me into staying. Some reached out over and over again. Others would no longer look me in the eye. It left me confused and searching for answers about how the church saw divorce. How they saw single moms. How they saw the children that were involved.

And over time, though there were some that did try to help, the ones that chose other paths were all I could think about. In my pain, my focus became skewed toward the negative.

Because I'd watched my church help others with problems that seemed far greater than mine. Others who approached them as the shell of a person I felt like, and grew to be restored. And yet all I seemed to do was fall apart more each day and wonder why God wasn't using the church I loved—the church I'd dedicated myself to—to heal me.

I began to slowly fade from the services. With the loss of my home, we had to move further from our church and it was nearly an hour away. I was no longer able to participate in weekly activities such as the Bible studies I once loved. At the same time, our women's ministry (which I was a leader in) fell apart and the women slowly lost contact with each other.

It was like the perfect storm during my already raging hurricane. It was the beginning of my faith slipping away from me. And I felt helpless as I watched it happen.

I began lashing out at God and everyone around me for what I was feeling toward anyone who I could associate with the church. I couldn't believe that something that I had poured my heart into helping others would somehow turn a blind eye to me when I was going through the worst time of my life. I was angry at everything they stood for and everything I had once believed about them.

Until one day this thought occurred to me:

What if what I had believed about them was not who they were meant to be in my life?

After a year or more of being disconnected from the church, when the pain of my loss had subsided a little and I was able to look back more objectively, I started to see past the bad experiences and realize the good ones were the ones I should have been focusing on. Like the wise and loving counselors who'd helped me work through my heartbreak. The friends from the women's ministry who shared their own stories of loss and encouraged me by showing me what my life could look like in the future if I chose my steps wisely during my grief.

As a whole, my church was not the problem, though there were some within it that compounded my grief. I began to look at "the church" as a whole—as in any Christian I'd come in contact with—and try to understand where my anger was coming from.

o A neighbor I'd introduced to that church and had gone out of my way to help during her time of need, had turned on me and spread rumors that were completely fabricated.

o A leader in the church who I'd trusted told me that what my ex had done was due to a diseased mind and should be overlooked, regardless of what it had done to the rest of the family.

o People in my local community—who were known to be Christians—were isolating me in social situations and aiding my ex in the harassment that nearly sent him to jail for a year.

o Research I'd done on Christian websites about divorce were filled with judgment and an uncomfortable piousness toward those in my situation, with no regard for what was happening in the marriage—only a demand to stay married.

The result of these combined experiences and many others with "the church" made me feel let down by God somehow. And I was letting these imperfect people—imperfect just like me—to get in between me and my relationship with God.

Have you unknowingly done the same?

It's Not Them, It's You

Nearly a year went by from the time I decided my church had done serious harm to my fragile heart until the time I returned with the humble realization that it wasn't them. Nearly a year before I realized that I wouldn't find my healing there. Because all of them don't make up the Church alone. They are not my God. And they are not my Healer.

I needed to reach toward God in my brokenness, and God alone.

The Bible talks about broken hearts specifically. And clearly tells us that God will heal those wounds.

He heals the brokenhearted and binds up their wounds.
Psalm 147:3 (NIV)

But before a wound can be healed, it has to be offered up. It has to be shown to the Healer, no matter how ragged and broken. When we do that, we show that we are willing to do our part in caring for the wound and give God permission to assess the damage. He knows best what it will take to make it better, and understands the type of binding necessary to bring true healing. But, we have to step toward healing first.

True healing can be found only in reaching out to the One who offers it. Without bitterness and resentment getting in the way. Without anger and blame for others. But with an earnest heart that wants to find it. And an open mind that will allow it.

The wound can't be healed when we hover over it in anger, hiding and protecting it from the world. Because that is what causes a wound to fester. To become infected. To cause further damage to the wounded than the initial wound.

Sweet friend, if you've been hurt by the church and are blaming your specific church—or the people in it—for your pain, maybe what you're actually feeling is more of a longing for healing that you can't seem to place.

Let's reconsider our position and turn to the One who has offered to bind our wounds, while forgiving those who may have tried with the best of intentions but didn't quite reach what you needed, or what God hoped they might be in your life. The church alone or as a whole can't heal us. And the sooner we realize that—and the fact that they were never meant to—the sooner we will find the clarity to reach toward the One who longs to.

Setting Boundaries with Others

As we reach back toward God and rebuild that relationship, we also need to look at those who have repeatedly hurt us and set some boundaries. Because a heart can't heal when it is still being bruised. And there may be relationships or acquaintances we are struggling to maintain when the truth is that those people can't play the role we'd like for them to in our lives and we need to stop allowing them access to it.

Not everyone who hurts us on this walk does it intentionally. Some mean well and simply fall short. But when you are repeatedly hurt by someone, whether intentional or not, it's well within your right to protect yourself. Not only within your right, but it's something you should do—no matter who they are.

In order to do that, you'll need to get your feet back under you. So, we're going to walk through what it looks like to get yourself grounded and in a position to take control back:

Step 1: Acknowledge Your Own Feelings

Your feelings matter. Acknowledging how you truly feel about a situation and the way you are being treated—not what someone has suggested you have the "right" to feel—is crucial to finding a solution. Spend time thinking through your feelings and the emotions that arise when you are in situations with the person or people you feel are causing you harm. Think about your natural reactions and actions when they are around you. Consider how you feel before and after each time you are with them. Get familiar with your own feelings and face the truth about them, then make decisions about how to move forward based on those truths.

Step 2: Drop the Guilt

It's hard when we recognize that someone we trust may not be good for us to have in our day-to-day lives. And while some people may hurt you, ask for your forgiveness and move forward in a positive relationship toward the future, others are not capable—or not willing—to do anything other than what they've always done to you. Their bad behavior is not your fault. And you don't owe them anything. Recognize that guilt for being the "bad guy" and pulling away from a bad situation could be the very thing that is keeping you there. And guilt is not a good enough reason to stay. You deserve more from the people you allow into your life.

Step 3: Set Boundaries

A person who has repeatedly shown you that they don't care about your well-being, and are only concerned with themselves doesn't deserve the same access in your life as someone who loves and cares for you. Though it's difficult to consider, there are times when you have to set boundaries with those you thought would never go against you. Standing up for yourself is necessary to your own emotional health, peace of mind, and safety. Set up boundaries that fit the situation you are dealing with. Physical abuse would obviously involve severe boundaries such as a complete removal of this person from your life. Whereas someone who is causing emotional harm during specific situations may lead you to only remove them from those specific situations. You have to guard your heart from those who would do irreparable harm, even if they are in your own family.

Step 4: Show Grace

Setting limits on someone who continually hurts you doesn't have to be an all or nothing venture. If you are able to, and think it could help in healing the relationship, try to be open to reconciliation in the future. Actions speak volumes. Try to show grace to those who are making a sincere and concerted effort to repair your relationship—but only if you see that being manifested by their actions and not empty promises.

If you are being hurt by someone you've allowed into any aspect of your life, you have every right to set parameters around that relationship. You should never stay in any relationship that is harming you, regardless of whether or not that person is a member of your own family. While some relationships may have to end, others can continue with a clear recognition of what you will and will not allow.

Coming Clean

Remember that list at the beginning of the chapter? I want you to spend a little time with it. Not much, because we are in the business of moving forward, past those things that are holding us back. But, we're going to face it. Face them. The people we feel have hurt us in this process.

I mentioned buying a journal in Chapter 2. We're not going to use that here. I want that journal to be something you look back at and cherish. I want it to be full of positive steps in your life that pull you out of your pit and towards a renewed relationship with God. So, don't forget to pick one up if you haven't already (and the cute pens!).

Single Mom Challenge 7:

I want you to set some time aside in the next 24 hours to come clean with the top 3 people on your list. Not in person—don't throw this book down and run away, lol—but through visualization. You can do this in the shower, in your bed at night, or when you're hiding from your kids in the bathroom. Anywhere you get a moment. But, I want you to focus on it because we're getting it out there once and for all.

We're coming clean, and cleaning house.

Start with the first person on your list. Visualize sitting across from them. They will be sitting calmly with their hands in their laps, and their mouths shut (no really, they will). As you begin, look them directly in the eye and tell them every single thing they've done that has hurt you and how it made you feel. Pour it all out, they're listening. Spill the beans. Make a mess.

If you have to whisper because little ears are nearby, whisper. If you need to scream at them, scream at them. But, make an audible noise. Don't just imagine talking in your head.

When you are done, stand up from your chair, nod your head at them, and leave.

You've just set a mental boundary, and we're sticking to it.

If you are able to start the next conversation, go into another room setting and do the same. If you need time to regain your composure first, wait and do so.

But, have those talks with your top three. They need to hear it. You need to say it. And then, we're moving on.

THE SINGLE MOM CHALLENGE

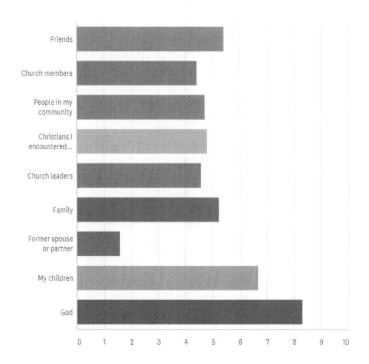

	Most Harm	Least Harm	Score	Rank Least to Most		List in order Least to Most
Friends	0	0	5.39	3		1 God
Church Members	2.53	0	4.42	8		2 My Children
People in my community	0	1.3	4.7	6		3 Friends
Christians I encountered	1.19	1.19	4.8	5		4 Family
Church Leaders	2.47	2.47	4.56	7		5 Christians I encountered
Family	3.8	3.8	5.22	4		6 People in my community
Former Spouse or Partner	84.69	3.06	1.6	9		7 Church Leaders
My Children	1.15	9.2	6.68	2		8 Church Members
God	2.2	82.42	8.31	1		9 Former Spouse or Partner

83

Chapter 5

Rebuilding Yourself

This was the hardest chapter for me to write. In fact, I wrote it last. Because of all the things I've struggled with as a single mom, rebuilding myself—my home, my finances, my self-esteem—has been one of the most difficult and emotional battles I've ever gone through.

This is also the most necessary chapter in the book. In fact, if we can't successfully navigate through this chapter and seek healing on the other side, we might as well use this book as a door stop. You know, the door to our future happiness. Because without seeking out and putting a concerted effort into healing the deepest wounds within us, we can't move forward toward what God has up ahead for us. We can't put a Band-Aid over it and pretend it's healed because the two most intimately involved parties — us and God — both know that is a lie and a cover-up.

And we're done with that kind of lifestyle. Am I right?

We're pushing toward the future baring our souls.

A few years ago, I read an article by another mom-blogger who talked about the day she stopped eating burnt toast. Though I can't recall the writer's name, I can recall with great clarity the feeling of *"Oh yeah, I should stop doing that too!"* that came over me as she detailed how she was tired of always giving herself the leftovers, the crumbs in life, the pieces of burnt toast.

But sometimes, it's hard to believe we deserve better.

Sometimes we're so focused on what everyone else needs, on what we are expected to do as a mom, on the people we would willingly lay our own lives down for, that we forget we matter too.

You matter too.

And while there is something to be said for sacrifice, and giving, and loving with grace, we are not called to ignore everything that happens to us — as if we don't matter — and just pretend that we are okay with being treated like the bottom of someone's shoe, for everyone else's sake.

85

It takes me back to where I often go when struggling with how I'm feeling about myself and what I may or may not "deserve" in this life: I think of my kids.

If one of them were in my situation, what would I want for them? To be shoved to the corner and their thoughts/feelings/needs ignored so that others could continue with the status quo? Or, to stand up and say — even if only in a strained whisper — *this is not working. This is not okay. This is not how I should be treated.*

Which also takes me to where I go next: I think of God and how I'm his kid. How he might look at my situation and think: Why is she trying so hard to be a martyr? Doesn't she know I need her to take care of herself first — so that she can take care of everything else I've given her? Doesn't she know her worth, and that I want only good things for her? Good — not harm? Doesn't she know that she isn't responsible for the brokenness in others? She's only responsible for healing and restoring herself to Me?

Do you know?

Do you know that though Jesus put God first in his life, He put Himself second? That even though He served like no one else in history, He never once took on another person's actions and thought — *yes, I deserved that because I put myself in the position to receive it.* He prayed for those that hurt Him, but he also stood up for Himself.

He rebuked injustice. He called people out of their sin. He freed us from ourselves, and didn't then say, *"But thou art responsible for every other bad thing that you allow to happen to you in life."*

Because sometimes we are treated unfairly. Sometimes horribly. Sometimes just carelessly.

But, we aren't called to stay there for the simple fact that we found ourselves there. Of course, the enemy loves to tell us otherwise. Because keeping us in a place where we feel broken, and helpless, and hopeless fuels his great desire for us: to make us feel stuck. Incomplete. Alone.

Sweet friend, you are anything but. The simple fact that you've held yourself in a place that's been hard for you speaks volumes to your heart for following what you believe God is calling you into. Just don't make the mistake of believing that He's calling you into another person's mistakes. He's not calling you to pay the price for another person's actions or sins. He gave us a Savior for that very purpose. Who reached into the lives of the broken and offered forgiveness and healing, and redemption. It's not something we can do for them. And, quite frankly, it's not what we're called to do.

Because you matter too.

Seeing Yourself for Who You Are

It's funny the baggage we carry through life while leaving other good things behind. The bad stuff really is easier to believe (thanks, *Pretty Woman*).

As Christians, we want to believe that God's grace is enough to cover everything we've done and everything that's been done to us. We strive to lay it down and let Him take it over. Maybe we've done that over and over again with

What, if anything, helped you heal from the loss of your relationship and being thrust into single-momhood?

In the movie Fried Green Tomatoes, Evelyn explains the healing nature of her relationship with the elderly Ninny Threadgoode as having someone in her life who "held a mirror up to her face." I had two friends who did this for me. As a Christian, I really struggled with a lot of guilt over getting divorced. I had experienced some withdrawal from my church family. My friends helped me see the gross unhealthiness of my marriage and face some of the destructive thought and behavior patterns in my own life. Having someone say, "You are more than your present version of yourself," really helped inspire me to fight for wholeness.

Caroline, single mom of 1, recently remarried

some things in our lives. We think we're doing just fine —
even if we're in a tough season — and we push through it
because everyone is telling us that He's got our back. That
God is good all the time. That we will have what we need
if we just believe.

But the truth is that if our struggle is long, we may
begin to waver in our hearts. We look at others on similar
journeys and are discouraged to see that ours has lasted so
much longer, or that our mountains rival Kilimanjaro
while theirs look like molehills. We might even feel shame
(or be shamed) for saying out loud that we're not sure God
actually IS in this with us. Because we feel left behind
somehow. Forgotten. Unnoticed.

I've been there.

In fact, it was in the midst of being there that I realized
something pretty unsettling about myself. Because while I
was faltering in my faith, struggling to consider that
everything I'd come to accept about God might not be
true, I was still on fire for Him when it came to others.
Others I cared about were going through difficulties of
their own — some so much harder than mine — and I had
no problem standing up for them, calling out to God, and
believing wholeheartedly that He would not only hear my
prayer, but would step in because of it. For them.

But me? I realized I felt exactly the same way with God
as I did as a child in a home that was full of turmoil. I felt

unheard. Forgotten. Pushed to the side so that more pressing matters could be handled.

That He would willingly come with swords blazing to the needs of everyone I cared about, but He might — just might — look at my situation, shrug His shoulders, and move on to something more important.

That's a little embarrassing to admit. But true.

Because in my heart of hearts, I'm still that little girl doing everything she can to measure up. To be seen. To do so many great things that everyone will notice. To follow every rule. To be good. So, so good that they will love her for it.

And apparently, deep down, I believe that I won't measure up for Him either. Even if I follow every rule. Even if I follow none of them and rely on His grace. At the end, I see myself standing before Him and hearing that He didn't really know me. As in, *He didn't really notice me at all.* Even when I clung to the belief that He would.

Do you struggle with the same?

Because we base our lives, our decisions, on our experiences. Do you base your beliefs about God on lessons learned by how others treat you?

The truth is, that's unfair towards God. Because no experience compares to that of our relationship with Him. He simply doesn't work that way. He doesn't react or behave like anyone we've ever known. And let's face it:

That blows our mind to the point that we can't even comprehend it.

He is grace-giving.

For it is by grace you have been saved, through faith—and this is not from yourselves, it is the gift of God— 9 not by works, so that no one can boast.

Ephesians 2:8-9 (NIV)

He is loving.

We love because he first loved us.

1 John 4:19 (NIV)

He is faithful.

If we are faithless, he remains faithful,
for he cannot disown himself.

2 Timothy 2:13 (NIV)

He is protective.

He will cover you with his feathers.
He will shelter you with his wings.
His faithful promises are your armor and protection.

Psalm 91:4 (NLT)

He is understanding.

"For my thoughts are not your thoughts, neither are your ways my ways," declares the Lord. "As the heavens are higher than the earth,

so are my ways higher than your ways and my thoughts than your thoughts.

Isaiah 55:8-9 (NIV)

He cherishes you.

"What is the price of five sparrows—two copper coins? Yet God does not forget a single one of them. And the very hairs on your head are all numbered. So don't be afraid; you are more valuable to God than a whole flock of sparrows."

Luke 12:6-7 (NLT)

He won't leave you.

I will not leave you as orphans; I will come to you.

John 14:18 (NIV)

He will never change.

"I the Lord do not change. So you, the descendants of Jacob, are not destroyed."

Malachi 3:6 (NIV)

And ... He doesn't show favoritism.

For God does not show favoritism.

Romans 2:11 (NLT)

If you believe that God's promises are true for other people, then that's enough faith to start with. Remember the mustard seed? You've got a little more than that. You just need to start reconciling your heart to the fact that – *yes* — He means you too.

Especially you.

Because if you were the only one He could save, He would still do it all over again.

Just for you.

He loves you that much.

Ask Him to help you know that you know that you know that His promises are meant for you too, without doubt. And you know what? He will.

<u>Single Mom Challenge 8:</u>

With your name/me/I/etc. replaced at the appropriate places, pick two verses that speak to you (from the list above or in your Bible) about your relationship with God and write them here. For example:

He will cover <u>*me*</u> with his wings; <u>*I*</u> will be safe in his care; his faithfulness will protect and defend <u>*me*</u>.

Verse 1:

_____

_____

_____

_____

_____

_____

_____

Verse 2:

_____

_____

_____

_____

_____

_____

_____

Record these in your journal.

Take Care of You

If I could have been born into a different family, I think I would have fit in well with a large Jewish clan. The mothers, I'm told, are masters at laying on the guilt. And I, sweet friends, am a sponge.

For as long as I can remember, I've never been able to put myself first without repercussions of serious guilt. If there was a last cookie on a plate, I couldn't eat it without feeling it should be someone else's. If there was extra money available to buy something I desperately needed, I still couldn't buy it without guilt. If there was a work trip that took me away for more than twenty-four hours—even though my job was providing for all of our needs—I'd feel terrible for leaving my kids.

As a mom, guilt followed me like a shadow, ready to taunt me at a moment's notice if my thoughts moved even one centimeter off of others and onto myself. When I became a single mom, that guilt somehow (as if it was even possible) magnified. And no matter how often I heard it, or how many voices in my life suggested it, I couldn't seem to put even the tiniest focus on myself.

On the selfish act of taking care of me.

Until one day, I went to pack for a work trip and realized that I didn't own a single pair of underwear that didn't have holes in them. And, I don't mean tiny ones from initial signs that I needed new ones. No. I mean, big, gaping, embarrassing holes that made them so ratty, they might have looked like lace from a distance. Ok, they didn't. But remembering it that way makes me feel better.

And it was that drawer full—and I mean full—of expired underwear, that made me realize the truth: though my family never had to worry about running out of toilet paper, milk, deodorant, clean socks, or bread, I was living as if I didn't deserve to have my basic needs met. As if taking care of me somehow took something away from someone I loved.

The real kicker? I realized the number of times I'd literally walked past the underwear aisle in my local Wal-Mart (hint: did you know that they sell it for just a few dollars?), perusing the aisles three to five times a week while locating items that the rest of my family needed— and didn't take care of my own needs.

Don't you realize that all of you together are the temple of God and that the Spirit of God lives in you?
1 Corinthians 3:16 (NLT)

I closed that drawer, determined that I had to start taking better care of myself. One look down the hallway would show three children who were continuing to grow, who would someday leave my home. When they did so, I didn't want to be a deflated balloon that they had spent 18 years sucking the life out of. Because leaving behind a

THE SINGLE MOM CHALLENGE

shell of the mother they once had, would only cause me to fill that empty space with mourning for what I'd just lost.

But, if instead, I began to fill myself up by taking better care of myself, becoming healthy both on the inside and the out, and even spoiling myself from time to time, I would still mourn the loss, but would have so much more to offer them as we each went into the next season of our lives together. I would be so full of other things I'd allowed into my life, that the passing of that season wouldn't consume me.

Sweet girls, don't buy into the lie of being selfish. We are called to take care of ourselves so that we can set out to do the work God has for us. We honor those we love when we respect ourselves enough to take care of our own needs (and sometimes wants).

So you know where I started?

With new underwear.

And you know what? It was the most fun-filled shopping trip I've ever had. Hands down. Because not only did I get rid of that drawer of undies-past-their-prime, but I got rid of the guilt. I refused to accept it anymore. And decided from that day forward that it was okay to take care of myself, to remember the things I once enjoyed, and even to make a plan that went beyond mothering my children.

And the undies? Some even had lace on them, people.
Actual. Lace.

<u>Single Mom Challenge 9:</u>

There's no better time than the present to take care of yourself. You've got too much ahead to neglect what's going to get you there. Make a list of the top 5 ways you've neglected taking care of yourself. And how you're going to change that.

Areas of my life that I've let go for far too long:

1._____

_____

2._____

_____

3._____

_____

4._____

_____

5._____

_____

5 Things I pledge to do to take care of me:

1. _____

   ☐_____ date completed

2. _____

   ☐_____date completed

3. _____

   ☐_____date completed

4. _____

   ☐_____date completed

5. _____

   ☐_____date completed

Transfer these to your journal.

Chapter 6

Rebuilding Your Children

The fact is, you were called to be a mom. How do I know that? Because you are one. No amount of planning on our part can create a child outside of God's will. If you have a child, it is in His will for you to be a mother. If the heavens parted and God handed you a pen and paper and said, "I have called you to write," you'd likely spend the rest of your life pursuing and relishing that word from Him. Sister, the heavens did open, and He handed you a child. You should react the same.

You've been given a position of influence in the lives of your children. In fact, if the truth be told, you are the single greatest influence in their life—regardless of their age. For me, the biggest part of that influence is my influence in their faith. We have such a small window of time to build their faith. And like most things, it's not built by our words, but by our actions. The last thing I want as a single mom is to somehow lead my children astray by the actions I'm taking during this most difficult time in my life. Because honestly, that could cause them to do the same during a future most difficult time in their lives.

And I don't want to be the reason they stumble, sisters.

Because the actions they witness us take today, are the same actions they will come to believe are okay for themselves in the future. We all know—don't we—of examples where we witnessed our own mothers doing something and then came to believe we could do the same. Maybe a bad behavior, or attitude toward something. Maybe an outlook on life, or the way she spoke to someone.

Because this is not just a momentous life change for us. It is for our children as well. And believe me, as a daughter who's walked through her parent's divorce, they are looking to you to build something they can live with in the future. The actions and attitudes we take now, will be the foundation our family moves on to from here.

Let's make it a strong one. Let's make it one that God has His hands in.

Letting Them In

If I were to round up just a small fraction of the single moms I've met in the past few years, we could literally spend hours cataloguing the combined losses we've suffered.

I bet you could too.

Dealing with loss as a mom can be extremely complicated. Because in the middle of our ugliest ugly, sometimes we've glanced to our side, or down the hall, or around the corner to discover our sweet children watching us—waiting to see if we're all going to make it through.

Sometimes we've held it together despite how we felt. And sometimes we've taken part in what can only be described as a glorious meltdown. You know, the one where we're crying so hard we can't catch our breath, and we're talking gibberish, and flailing our arms, and slimy things start flowing from our faces.

Just me? Ahem.

It's during these bouts of uncontrollable anguish— when I've typically hidden in the bathroom, or the nearest closet, or even my car—that I've struggled deeply with this question:

Should we let our children see our pain?

At first glance, the sides are split.

Side 1: Of course we should, we're not robots. For children to truly know and appreciate their mother, it's okay for them to see the human side of her at times.

Side 2: Of course we shouldn't, we should protect them from our personal suffering and losses. They are too young to deal with such things and it's irresponsible to burden them.

Maybe you stand with side 1. Maybe you stand with side 2. Or, maybe you're caught in between the two. As I was considering this while writing, I decided to consult other single moms on The Christian Single Mom Facebook page and asked these two questions:

Should you allow your child to see you crying about the break-up of your marriage?
- o   No
- o   Yes, I'm only human.
- o   Yes, but only on rare occasions when I can't avoid it.
- o   I'm not sure.

Has your child seen you crying over the break-up of your marriage?

o No

o Yes, I didn't try to hide it.

o Yes, but I did everything I could to hide it.

The results were fascinating to me.

Out of 93 surveyed, 47% said yes we should let our children see us cry—we're only human, and 40% said yes but only when it's unavoidable. 6.5% weren't sure, and 6.5% said no.

But, even with 87% of single moms surveyed agreeing that we should allow our children to see us grieve the loss, 47% stated that their children had seen them grieving even though they tried everything they could to hide it.

They're torn, just like me. Just like you in all likelihood.

It's a hard thing to manage—these raging emotions while trying to protect our children from further pain. Because make no mistake about it, they are grieving too, whether we see them cry or not.

Speaking from both sides of this issue, I can tell you firsthand that I've been that child watching my mother struggle through the loss of a marriage. Through the crushing reality that her dream for her family had been shattered. I've watched my mother suffer hopelessly, while those who should have stood beside her were nowhere to be found. And it's one of the most heartbreaking parts of my childhood.

Heartbreaking.

Because in the midst of her pain, I wanted to be the one to make it better. I wanted to see her happy again. And I wanted to know that she was going to be okay. That we were all going to be okay.

And so I began to play a part. A role that pushed my feelings to the floor for the sake of my mother. A role that showed her how happy I was for the smallest things because I couldn't bear to bring her one more moment of unhappiness, or to make her take on my own. It didn't help at the time that every other adult in my life was pretending as if nothing had happened. Because just as everyone had abandoned my mother, everyone who could have stepped in to help me walked away too.

I just remember these simple truths from that period of my life:

o   No one asked how I felt about it
o   No one asked if I was okay with the enormous amount of change coming my way
o   No one asked about what I had experienced

Please understand that I'm not placing blame. I've been through unfathomable grief as my own marriage fell apart. Grief that literally held me to the ground some days. I can completely understand how my mother didn't have the presence of mind to be able to rally around us. But being able to see the other side now, made me think long and hard through each and every move I made with my children as I suffered through my own grief.

And I think that's how it should be. Each mother should thoughtfully consider her actions and gauge what her children are ready for as the family grieves the loss.

The truth is somewhere in the middle of these two sides:

There's a time for concealing our pain. And there's a time for sharing it with them.

And both can be done while showing our children the utmost respect during what will come to be known as one of the most difficult times in their lives.

Hide and Seek

In the beginning, I hid everything from my children. I never let myself forget the simple truth that they were also in pain from the loss of their family. And I have a deep, deep respect for that. I wasn't in the right frame of mind to be able to sit down and share with them in a way that was healthy or didn't place an undue burden on them—and so I didn't.

But, as time passed and I got my footing as a single mom (and I don't mean years, I mean weeks. In other words, just got to my feet), I came to the realization that while no mother should ever expose their children to too much of their story of loss, it also does them a great disservice when we don't allow them to see us grieving the loss. Because while they are watching us closely to see if we are all going to get through this to the other side, they are also watching to see if it's okay and acceptable to show us the pain they are in too.

So, as I've continued to travel down this path, I've let my children in on a little secret: their mother is human and she is deeply saddened (just as they are) about what happened to our family. And I've encouraged them to share their grief as well.

The truth about this journey as a single mom is that we are never alone on our path because we are mothers. And as much as we might feel the urge to hide our pain from our children and pretend that life is still exactly the same as before, it will never be the same for either of us. They know that. They grieve that loss deeply. But, they are looking to where we will lead them next.

It's our job to teach them that it is okay and entirely possible to grieve something in your past, and then look forward and start building your future. In reality, this is a gift we are giving them that not many children will

THE SINGLE MOM CHALLENGE

receive. We are showing them in real time what it looks like to start over while dealing with a painful and devastating loss. We are teaching them firsthand how to overcome.

It's time to hit reset, Mama. We're prepping them for more. Let's walk through how to do that.

Building Solidarity

It's an unfortunate truth in society that half of children today will go through the break-up of their family, and their parent's divorce. Though it's obviously not God's ideal, it does happen, and needs to be approached with grace from not only those on the outside, but those on the inside.

One of the biggest mistakes parents make while going through a divorce or break-up is leaving the children out of the conversation. While this may seem counterintuitive, think about it: they have suffered a loss as well, are grieving as well, and need someone to work through it with them as well.

Being open (in general, no child needs or wants to know the down-and-dirty-specifics of their parents' marriage, break-up, or divorce) about the situation, what decisions you are facing as a family, and how things will move forward helps to build a sense of solidarity between you and your children. You are in this together. You will make decisions (to a point) together. And most importantly, you will build something new and uniquely beautiful, together.

Think about it: what's the one thing you longed for the most as you've gone through the breakup of your family? I would bet large amounts of chocolate that it was simply someone to go through it with you. Someone who stood by you. Someone who listened and made every effort to understand and support you no matter what. Am I right?

You can be that for your children.

Bring it Up

As a parent, it's your job to discuss the tough issues with your child no matter how difficult. But before you do, make sure you put things in perspective with three simple ground rules:

1. Don't make it about you. Allow them to talk about their pain without bringing your own into it.
2. Don't speak negatively of your ex. No matter how hard the urge to do so is (and believe me, it will be incredibly difficult), they don't need guilt piled on top of their pain.
3. Don't allow them to leave with a negative mindset. Clear the air.

They need to talk about it. But they will never be the first to bring it up. They are aware of the pain that surrounds the situation and are putting on a brave face for the simple fact that they love you.

So, bring it up. Ask how they feel about it. Continue with questions until the conversation is exhausted, paying attention to body language that might suggest that they are hiding how they truly feel. They desperately need to get it off their chest.

Give them the grace to do so.

Give them a Free Pass
Don't limit them during the discussion. No matter their age, they have a right to understand as much as they want to. They have been hurt, and deserve to have their questions answered if at all possible. If there are tough reasons behind the end of the relationship, be prepared to give a thoughtful answer that is at their level of understanding. Showing them that they have a right to ask about it will alleviate fear and anxiety, and make them see that their feelings matter to you. This builds trust. Be prepared for difficult emotions to surface, and allow them to express those as much as possible.

Be Vulnerable
There's nothing wrong with showing weakness to your child. If you are in pain, it's okay to express that. The entire

family is going through a huge loss. Don't pretend to have it all together if you are struggling, while keeping in mind that your child is not your therapist. It's fine to express your sadness about the divorce, that you wish things had happened differently, and any other things you may be feeling that could build a common bond between you as you grieve this loss together.

Be Ready to Apologize

Regardless of the reasons behind your marriage's demise, your children have been hurt through no fault of their own. And like any situation where we are hurt by someone, regardless of whether the hurt was intentional or not an apology can begin the healing process. Apologize to your child for the situation that they find themselves in and encourage them to express their anger or fear over being hurt. Again, don't place blame on your ex here. Even though the marriage may have dissolved due to something that was out of your control, this is not the time to point that out. Earnestly apologize. Nothing more.

Give them a Voice

Don't make life decisions moving forward that completely exclude your child. Of course, you are the parent and will have the ultimate decision in where you now live, if you move onto another relationship, etc. But, give your child the chance to voice their opinion. Ask them how they feel and what they think about any plans moving forward that might mean change for them. Even if you can't fix their feelings, or do things the way they would prefer, the fact that you respected them will go a long way.

While these conversations are never easy, they can actually be a bonding moment in which pent-up grief is shared, your hearts are open to one another, and understanding is built between you. Your child was an integral part of the prior family unit and deserves the same respect you would want if major life changes were on your horizon. When they express difficulties they are having with the changes in their life, don't simply brush them off because they are a child. They are valid points and meaningful to them or they wouldn't have brought them to your attention. You should consider them just as you will one day want them to consider your feelings and position in other family matters.

Your new version of family can be even stronger than the original. The very fact that your family is no longer together suggests that there were unhealthy situations that would have made it impossible for you to actually have the loving, close, fun family experiences you always dreamed you would have.

Those days are not lost.

In fact, the best version of the relationships with your children can be up ahead. And this is your opportunity to make a radical change in that direction. Let's help rebuild our children, lifting them up from this upset in their life, toward a new version of family that they will look back on fondly for the rest of their lives.

> **What is one piece of advice you would give a new single mom about the journey she has just begun?**
> Spend time with your children helping them to learn to enjoy the life they now must live. They hurt, too, and are confused by the changes in their parents' priorities. Also, find something that is just yours, some activity that you can focus on at least once a week, and do it. I joined the community chorale.
>
> Barbara, single mom of 5

***

I think it's also important to address the unique needs that individuals go through in the loss of the family. Your children's loyalties are now torn because their parents are

THE SINGLE MOM CHALLENGE

no longer one. If your relationship with your ex is strained, your children may worry that the feelings you have toward your ex, the way you see your ex, or the issues you have with your ex will somehow rub off on them or become your issue with them. This is a real fear. And one that you shouldn't brush over.

Rebuilding Your Son

A son's relationship with his mother is a unique one. A beautiful one. One that sets the tone for all of his other relationships in the future. It's how he'll learn to express his emotions, how he'll understand women, and how he'll view himself. When that son has a single mother, it offers an entirely different set of challenges. Make sure your son knows you believe these things about him as well:

You see him as a unique individual. Parting ways with your child's father, no matter how that happens, is often filled with much pain and possible resentment. As a child, your son will assume that you associate him with his father for no other reason than they are the same sex and he likely associates himself that way (just as you likely did with your mother). Give your son the gift of not only recognizing him as a unique individual apart from his father, but acknowledging that you see him that way. Comparing him to his father may seem complimentary at times, but should you struggle to maintain a positive relationship with the other parent, your child will remember the comparison in a negative way and worry that you feel the same negativity toward him.

You believe he will be an honorable man. Let's face it, there aren't many heroes in today's world. Examples of good, kind men are few and far between. Yet, it is these kinds of qualities that can make a difference in your child's life as an adult. Instilling the belief that you see these qualities in your own son, will help him understand what he needs to strive toward. Build up his awareness of his faithfulness, goodness, kindness, courage, humility, strength, and hardworking character, and you'll see him respond in exactly those ways.

You believe he will be an amazing father. Whatever the circumstances are between you and your son's father, again, your son will already compare himself to his dad. If he feels that his father is not succeeding in this role, he may begin to feel that he too will not be successful in it. Point out the things he does as he grows that would suggest his ability to be an outstanding father (being kind to younger siblings, for example) and let him know that he already possesses the qualities he needs to succeed.

You want him to have a good relationship with his father. For many single moms, nothing is more challenging than maintaining a good relationship with their child's father. Truly, it's in everyone's best interest that this is as positive as it can be. However, the reality is that it doesn't always work as we'd like it to. Regardless of the difficulty or ease, make sure that you are sincere in your efforts to help your child navigate a positive relationship with their father.

You want him to be all boy. The daily struggle to stay afloat as a single mom can lead us to keep a tight ship because it seems like the only way to make it. However, do not forget to allow space for the simple things your son needs like the joy of playing rough and getting dirty. Join your son outside, or send him with friends, and encourage him to play hard, get dirty, and enjoy that side of boyhood that we simply don't understand at times. Make sure you show him how much you value this side of his personality and that it's not only accepted, but celebrated.

Single mothers have the toughest job on the planet, hands down. When you are raising a son as a single mom, additional challenges will surely arise, but you have everything you need to do it successfully. Keep an eye on the prize: a godly man of character. Build your son toward that goal every chance you get.

Rebuilding Your Daughter

There's no relationship on earth more complicated than that between a mother and her daughter. There's also the potential for something incredible. More than anyone else in our lives, daughters keep a close eye on everything we do. They are learning how we honor being a woman, how we treat others, and how we let others treat us with the idea that they should mimic our behavior. No matter their age, while they are still in our homes, they idealize us to a point. They admire who we are. And they want to pick the parts they find pleasing and duplicate those in their own lives. Make sure your daughter knows you believe these things about her:

You see her as a unique individual. When your marriage ended, your exes level of respect for you, your feelings, and your needs probably plummeted. Since your daughter associates herself so much with you, she will worry that her father will do the same for the simple fact that you are the same sex. Give your daughter the gift of recognizing her as an individual by reinforcing that her relationship with her father is completely separate from yours, and that she need not worry about comparisons from either side. Comparing her to you (or allowing others to do so) may be flattering at times, but should you have a difficult relationship with your ex, she will begin to worry that she will also have a difficult relationship with him or that he will hold your similarities against her. She is her own person, celebrate that.

You believe she will make wise life choices. Regardless of how we became single moms, our children will look at our situation and consider how the decisions we made in our lives put us into that position. And while it's not typically as cut and dry as one decision, children often see things in black and white. Make sure your daughter knows that you value her wisdom and believe that she is capable of making honorable choices in life that will lead her on the path God has chosen for her. The fear of making the same mistakes our parents made can often cause those things to come to fruition in our own lives. Don't be afraid to talk to her about life choices you made that were unwise and how she can learn from others experiences without going through them herself.

She is worthy of respect. More than anything, young women seek out relationships for validation. If we show them that we are willing to put up with bad behavior in a relationship, they are more likely to allow the same. Set a high bar for any relationships you bring into your home (whether these are girlfriends, family, or dating relationships).

She is to be cherished. While this may sound sexist, the desire to be taken care of is innate in women. No amount of equality can replace the need to find a mate that places our best interests above their own. It's how God intended us to be in relationship. And the fact that we are single mothers would suggest that our last relationship did not honor us in this way—and our children witnessed it. I want better for my daughter. Reassure your daughter that this is a noble quality in a man that she should seek out in any relationship she moves forward with in the future. We aren't meant to conquer the world alone, or to have to fight for someone to place us in a cherished position in their life.

You want her to have a good relationship with her father. Teach your daughter to honor the relationship with her father. Our daughters will associate many of their future relationships to their relationship with their father. It's in everyone's best interest to maintain a positive relationship if at all possible. If this relationship is strained however, help your daughter to understand that a parent's opinion—while important—is never more important than God's. Regardless of the difficulty or ease, make sure that you are sincere in your efforts to help your child navigate a positive relationship with their father.

How we handle our lives as a single mom is critical for our daughters. Because they are witnessing us as a single woman, they are also learning how to be a single woman, how to date, and how to handle life in general from us. Keep an eye on the prize: a godly woman of character. And help her see that in herself every chance you get.

Single Mom Challenge 10:

Make time to have the talks you need to have with your children so that you can walk through this season as a team, not divided. Plan those talks and record the dates here, or indicate that you have done this in the past.

I will talk to my children by

_____ (date).

I had an individual conversation with each of my children as shown here:

1. _____

    on _____(date)

2. _____

    on _____(date)

3. _____

    on _____(date)

4. _____

    on _____(date)

5. _____

    on _____(date)

Transfer these to your journal.

Show Them How

At the end of the day, more than anything else I teach my children, more than the fact that I want them to know that their mother is healthy and that we are all going to be okay, I want them to know this:

In my darkest struggle, I turned to God, and He carried me through it.

I want them to see that despite the pain, and heartache, and desperation they may one day experience in their own lives—even if they experience loss beyond what they think they can handle—they can turn to Him as well, and He will carry them through it.

I want them to remember that when they hurt, they don't need to do so alone. That it is better to come together and help each other through hard times. That family was built for that purpose.

And I want them to begin to recognize that inside of me—and each of them—is the remaining flicker of a light that can push us forward toward healing. No matter how tiny a spark it may seem at the time. And it has power that heals.

That flicker is burning inside of you too. And inside each of your children.

I know that because you have taken a chance with this book hoping for connection with God. Hoping for healing. He won't let you down.

We now have this light shining in our hearts, but we ourselves are like fragile clay jars containing this great treasure. This makes it clear that our great power is from God, not from ourselves.

2 Corinthians 4:7 (NLT)

Should you allow your child to see you crying about the break-up of your marriage?

Answered: 93   Skipped: 0

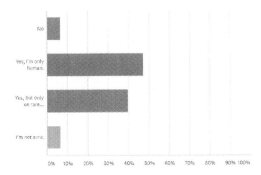

Has your child seen you crying over the break-up of your marriage?

Answered: 93   Skipped: 0

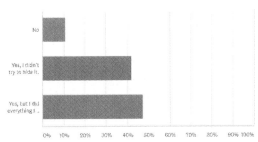

Chapter 7

Rebuilding Your Relationship with Your Ex

"I don't know how you do it all," she smiled at me in an attempt to encourage. "I could never handle all of that. You know, being both the mom and dad to my kids."

I stared at her a moment too long, creating an uncomfortable silence between us. A flash of panic flickered through my mind: *was I supposed to be both the mom and dad?*

We've all heard the concept before. Maybe even seen it in action from other single moms before we became one ourselves. At ball fields throwing baseballs, at scout meetings pitching tents, and at dance recitals carrying flowers to the stage.

But for me personally, I'd witnessed it firsthand as a child. I watched as my own mother struggled to make up for the hole that was left by my father. Listened as she told me that he still cared about me—even when it was clear he'd moved on. At my wedding—the day he officially disowned me—I felt numb as she spoke encouraging words about how much I meant to everyone *else*. How it was his loss, not mine.

By the time I became a single mom, I'd had a lifetime of watching others rush to fill the father gap in their children's lives. For many years it made me sick to witness—too close to what had happened to me. Until the day I finally realized that they were all missing the point. Because the truth is this:

1. We can't control our children's relationship with their father.
2. We are not called to fill the gaps in our children's lives.

Luckily for some, they don't have to. Their children's fathers fall in step with the new situation and do everything they can to be there, to comfort, and to provide a positive experience for everyone. But for others, their children's fathers fall to the wayside. Slowly pulling away, slowly fading in the time they spend, and slowly creating a rift between themselves and the rest of the family.

If you are one of the lucky few to find yourself in a positive situation with your ex, I'm honestly thrilled for you. That is a rare gift and I wish it were one that every single mom were given. But, this chapter is written with the other kind of relationship in mind. This chapter is going to delve into the difficult parts of having an ex and how we can still manage to glorify God despite what is going on there.

If you find yourself in the latter situation—the one where you are struggling with your ex in a myriad of ways—I want you to hear me now:

God has a plan for this.

You are Called to Be Their Mother

We were never called to be both the mother and the father to our kids. We were made their mothers. The very day our children came to being. Mothers. With enough responsibilities in that one word to build a lifetime around. Mothers. Who are gifted at loving, and caring for, and raising our children with the influence that only a mother can give.

We were never meant to be their fathers.

Seriously. Stop trying to do both.

Just be you.

Because the fact of the matter is that they already have a father. And whether that relationship is a positive one or a negative one, it is in their lives as little or as much as it is supposed to be. Because God saw this life you and your children would lead before it ever came to be. He knew your children's hearts, and wants, and needs. And He can use all of it for their good.

Every single bit.

He tells us so in Romans:

And we know that God causes everything to work together for the good of those who love God and are called according to his purpose for them.

Romans 8:28 (NLT)

He can take everything that happens in our lives—everything—and use it for good. Because regardless of how our earthly fathers act and react on this earth, we have Him. He claims us, in His own words:

"And I will be your Father, and you will be my sons and daughters, says the LORD Almighty."

2 Corinthians 6:18 (NLT)

We should encourage the very best relationship we can with our children and their fathers—it's our duty as their mothers. We shouldn't try to replace, or hinder, or especially excuse this role because it is pivotal in how they will one day grow in their relationship with others and with God. Doing so is manipulating the situation instead of letting God work through it.

But, if our children's father chooses not to be involved or falters, God Himself is already there filling the gap. God Himself will teach your child. God Himself will discipline your child. God Himself will guide your child.

How do I know this?

He did it for me.

He'll do it for your children as well.

When a Father Doesn't Step Up

Most people I know have no idea how I grew up.

That I was a little girl intent on earning her father's love. That I spent hours wishing things were different. That I studied other little girls—the good ones—to try to figure out what they did that made their daddies love them so much. And that I failed miserably at that feat— even to the point of being disowned.

It seems shocking to most, that a father could do that. That a young woman could bear that. And even more so, that she didn't then let it define the rest of her life.

But, they just don't understand that some fathers will purposefully choose not to parent. Some fathers will purposefully choose not to support their children. Some fathers will purposefully choose not to offer love to their children.

I can't tell you the precise moment I realized that my father didn't love me, but I can tell you that I struggled for 26 years trying to be good enough to change whatever was wrong with me.

It was a never-ending battle.

Hoping I would be smart enough, or funny enough, or maybe even cute enough to not only garner his attention, but his love.

His actual love.

To hear an "I love you" or an "I'm so proud of you" or even an "I'll always be there for you." But the words never came. Neither did the feelings behind them as I suffered for years under his scrutiny, disappointment, and public shuns. Until finally a day came when he made the break I knew he'd been wanting to make since day one:

He disowned me.

You see, after my parent's difficult divorce I grew very close to my stepfather. He was a loving man. An accepting man. A man who treated me as his very own. My relationship with my own father was strained to say the least. And when I became engaged, I wanted both my stepfather and my father to walk me down the aisle. One to support me, and the other out of respect.

When I told my father over lunch that I wanted both of them involved, the screaming began:

o *I'll never forgive you!*
o *You are no longer my daughter!*
o *You will regret doing this for the rest of your life!*

As every single eye in the restaurant turned to look at me, I could only imagine what they thought I'd done.

A few months later he made it official when not only he didn't show up for my wedding, but neither did another person from his side of the family. Not. One. He'd convinced them all to disown me as well. The same side of the family I'd spent every holiday with, every celebration, every summer break. Half of the people I'd loved my entire life—gone in an instant.

I don't know any other way than the path that God gave me. But, I can tell you that as a child, it was painful to watch my other friends with their fathers and wonder why mine couldn't just love me too.

As a young woman, I cried at weddings—not because of the love shared between the couple—because there were daddies that were sad to see their daughters leaving.

And I spent years of my life looking at myself in the mirror, and searching my heart to figure out what it was about me that made it so easy for him to hate me.

I mean, a Daddy is supposed to love his children unconditionally, right? It's innate. A part of being a parent. As mothers, we love our children so outrageously that we didn't even know that kind of love existed in our hearts until they came to be. Surely all parents feel the same.

Except when the love doesn't come.

I'll never know the answer to the questions I have about him. But, my heart is no longer crushed over my father's lost love. Because along the difficult path—about 30 years in—after bad choices in men, my career, my friends, how I treated my family, and even how I viewed my finances—

I met someone.

Introduced to him by two women from work, I was mesmerized by this man they spoke so highly of. This man who thought like no other. This man who came to set women like me free.

They knew Jesus intimately, and I wanted the same.

As I began to grow in my faith, and understand that I had a heavenly Father who loved me regardless of how my earthly father felt about me, I have to say it sent shockwaves through me. I'd never understood God in that way. In fact, the God I'd heard about was a whole lot like my father: he doled out love when I was good, and ripped it away when I wasn't.

Now I know that misconception is the farthest thing from the truth.

This Father I barely knew found me lovely and precious and cherished me as if I was His only daughter. He began working on the open wound my earthly father had crafted for years, and healed me completely by simply loving me.

Just loving me.

God will do the same for your child.

He will love on them, lead them, teach them, and show them that He's proud of them. He will talk with them, and reprimand them, and be there when no one else will for them. He will pull in when others pull away, and never leave them. Because more than they are a part of you and your ex, they are a part of Him—more fully than we can understand this side of heaven.

So do the right thing with your ex. Honor your children by giving them the opportunity to build that relationship. But, if like me, that relationship never comes to fruition, all is not lost. Because they have another Father in their lives that is ready to step in.

You do the part you were called to do. He will take care of the rest.

When You Can't Get Along no Matter What You Do

People will tell you who they are. Both literally, and by their actions. The hard part is believing them. We want to expect more. We want them to overcome the negative in our minds. We want them to be what we need them to be in our lives. But, people will tell you who they are.

While I truly believe that building a good relationship with your ex is important, this chapter isn't a lesson on things to do or steps to take to make that happen. Because more often than not, that relationship is strained and extremely difficult. The fact that you are no longer with your ex is proof that the relationship was not manageable.

So instead, you may need to do some emotional damage control.

In a perfect world, there would be no such thing as an ex. People would love like they are meant to, marriages would thrive and love would win every time. But in the broken world we actually reside in, life throws punches. Sucker punches at times. And we find ourselves single and maneuvering our children through waters we never even wanted to dip our toes into.

In the beginning of this second season of singleness, we often have high hopes of how things will go. We're all adults, after all. We can all place our differences aside for the sake of the children. We can be kind to one another for the sake of the children. We can respect one another moving forward, for the sake of the children.

Except when we can't.

And while I'm a strong proponent of doing everything you can to get along with, respect and not disparage your ex, sometimes the other party isn't willing to cooperate. Sometimes you are placed in a situation in which no amount of trying on your end matters. There are some people in life that you just won't be able to get along with. If that person happens to be the parent of your child, it can be heartbreaking to realize the uphill battle they are forcing you to fight.

What was your number one fear for your children as a single mom?

I was worried about how my daughter would develop without a father. I knew she would have role models, male friends and family members, but who knows how that compares to the hands on father? I also had to deal with her self-esteem as she grew up with no contact from her father. The question of why he didn't love her. My standard answer was that if he knew her he would love her.

Ruth, single mom of 1

But the truth is that having someone who insists on being contentious in our lives still doesn't define the relationship. You can only control one person in this world: YOU. You just need to realize what that looks like in this new version of your family.

In the midst of our difficulties, God gives us the power to bear the pain of unjust suffering. And while we may feel like the next step we should take is retaliation, we shouldn't. That's living by the world's standards. Not God's. And there is no better way to glorify the God we love than to give up, and ask Him to fight for us instead.

Not fighting may be one of the most difficult things you have to do. But, as much as it's in your ability to do so, you should turn the other cheek unless you or your children are in imminent danger.

This can look like a lot of unpleasant things:
- Ignoring the bad things being said about you.
- Letting the under-the-breath comments go.
- Ignoring the hurtful reaction when you ask for something that is well within your right to ask for.
- Letting the too-late-to-make-a-difference kindnesses pass over you, rather than remind you of all the times they couldn't offer them before.
- Ignoring the hurtful ways extended family now treats you.

Just typing those out makes me want to slap someone. Seriously. It's innate. It's human. But, it's not what we're called to do as believers. This is when we have to call on something bigger than us—stronger than us—to step in and take over before we make a mess of things.

Because in the long run, the mess we are making is not in our own lives, but in our children's. Most likely, we will move on to other relationships and maybe even a new marriage. We'll get to start over fresh in that regard. But our children's lives are being spelled out before them—right in front of them—though they have no say or control.

If we create a hostile environment—they will be the ones to suffer into adulthood.

If we disparage the other parent—they will be the ones to look within themselves and find something wrong.

If we let our anger rule our day-to-day lives—they will be the ones to lose their childhood.

So, don't be so quick to draw that line in the sand—even though it feels like exactly what you should do. Doing so only further separates a family that is already broken.

If it is possible, as far as it depends on you, live at peace with everyone.

Romans 12:18 (NIV)

As far as it depends on you, sweet friend. Control the things you can control, like these:

Don't disparage the other parent.

Even when you are being trashed by the ex, don't play in this sandbox. Because while it feels good to throw sand into the face of someone who's hurt you, the only ones who really get hit are the children. As a child who went through this herself, I can testify to the fact that your children will remember your actions. So at least try to take the high road long after the harsh words have been said against you. They will remember who fought fairly and who made your life (and theirs) unnecessarily difficult in an already hard situation.

Do defend yourself.

If things are being said to your children that are untrue or exaggerated, you have every right to respectfully point out the truth. Living a life of honesty goes a long way. Despite the things being said about you, children are smart and often read people much better than adults do. They can distinguish someone who is doing right from someone who is doing wrong. Be consistent in living an honest life and they will see that's who you really are.

Do protect yourself and your children.

You don't have to, and absolutely shouldn't, allow anyone to harass or emotionally (or especially physically) abuse you or your children. If this is occurring, it's your duty to limit and/or remove contact. Keep notes on what is going on, and if necessary, get authorities involved if the situation is keeping you and your children from being able to move on with a normal life.

Don't feel guilty for another person's choices.

It's easy to want to rectify any wrongdoing you feel is occurring from your ex. But remember, we *are* actually all adults here — even if not everyone is choosing to act that way. If they are making choices that cause problems or harm to you or your children, that is 100 percent on them, not you. If you are worried that things being done are setting your children up for future bad behaviors, you can assure your child that while their parent is usually a good person, they are currently making bad choices that you don't support and won't allow them to make.

Do involve your children in your relationship goals with your ex.

Let them know that your goal is to get along well with your ex, and to encourage a positive relationship between them and their other parent. Just as children have issues with their own friends, they understand that sometimes people just can't get along for periods of time. If you are in a period of not getting along with your ex, let your children know that you are doing the best you can and that you hope that it will resolve itself over time.

Do continue to move on with your new life.
No matter what occurred to end your marriage, the fact is that it's over and you deserve to move on and rebuild. Don't let an ex's behavior hold you back or make you feel like moving on is simply too much trouble. While it may be easier to lay low and hold back from life in order not to create waves, you will simply be choosing less than what life has to offer — a choice you likely were already accepting before you became a single parent. It's okay to live your life. It's okay to move on. Start the rebuilding process despite the difficulties so that you aren't allowing even more losses in your life or sabotaging your future.

Do pray for your Ex.
Regardless of how you feel about this person, how they are treating you, or their bad behavior, they — quite honestly — need the love of Christ more than anything else. Pray for them to find peace. Pray for them to grieve the loss well. Pray for them to rebuild or build their relationship with God. Truly, that is something we would do for others. Especially when they feel like an enemy in our lives.

Single parenting is hard. And while most of us want to do it to the best of our ability, we can't control the actions of the other parent in our children's lives. It's okay. We are only called to get along with someone to the best of our ability, *as far as it depends on us.* Make it your goal to do everything you can on your side of the relationship, while maintaining boundaries. Remember: You can only control the actions of one person in this world--yourself. Set goals and do your best to live at peace.

<u>Single Mom Challenge 11:</u>

You just wanted to punch me, didn't you? When I suggested you pray for your ex. If not, you likely have an excellent relationship and are doing just fine. But, most of us have spent years upon years trying to redefine a relationship that we don't want to be a part of anymore. We've thrown ourselves under the bus at times. We've butted heads. We've backed down. We've given up.

I know this is hard. But, if your relationship with your ex is so difficult that you can't earnestly pray for them, it's likely because you see them as someone who is still harming you—someone much like an enemy. And we all know what Jesus teaches about those guys, right? Pray for them.

But I say, love your enemies! Pray for those who persecute you!
Matthew 5:44 (NLT)

List three things that you could pray for your ex:

1. _____

2. _____

3. _____

THE SINGLE MOM CHALLENGE

Spend time praying to God about the difficulties you may have doing this, and ask for wisdom as to why you struggle, and what you can do to ease that.

Pray for each of the things you listed:

Item 1   □ completed on _____

Item 2   □ completed on _____

Item 3   □ completed on _____

Record these things, and how you felt before and after in your journal. And, congrats, sweet friend. That is a HUGE step you just took there.

Leaving it Behind with Grace

When we step forward and take the hand of God on this journey, that's huge. It might be the most difficult twelve inches you've ever trekked. You might be hardheaded and not want to. You might be angry and would rather step back. You might be heartbroken and can't make your feet move at all. In all of these situations, there are things we're still pulling behind us that we need to leave behind.

But we need to choose those things wisely.

Hurt and struggling to heal. Misunderstood and feeling alone. Facing a new normal that includes sharing our children—when our children are the only thread we are hanging onto. It's very tempting to want to push everything else behind us, swallow hard, and move forward. The world encourages it. Our friends encourage it. Even the legal system encourages it.

In some ways, it's a good idea. There's likely a tremendous amount of pain that can only be healed by the sweet release that comes with time and distance. But, as we're letting go, we need to make sure that we don't also leave the good behind—and pretend it was never there—for our children's sake. Because their future is also shaped by their past. Their genetic makeup is made of two parents. And a time will come in their lives when they will look back and consider the parts of each of their parents, and how a tiny bit of each is also a part of them.

If we've made those parts out to be horrible, or a mistake, or something unforgivable—it wounds no one more than it wounds our children. That's why as we let the hurt go and leave it behind, we need to do it with grace. We need to examine where we've been, how we got there, and the role that we played in it. We need to search for the good that might also have been there at some point in our past. We need to remember the moments of joy without allowing our current circumstances to taint them. And—hold onto your big girl panties—we need to recall the parts of our previous partner that were good, maybe even admirable, so that when our children ask about them we have answers that will show respect to our children.

We not only need to heal, but our children do as well. So that what we are leaving behind doesn't leave a scarlet thread tied to the past, called bitterness.

Because we will always be family. And as a family, we need to leave this breaking point behind us in a healthy way. So that everyone can move past it and not allow it to define our futures. In fact, one of the greatest gifts we can leave behind for our children—even though their original family is no longer intact--is a legacy of failure that was healed by forgiveness.

So they can see that forgiveness—true forgiveness—does exist, because they've witnessed it firsthand. They've lived through it. And that when it's coupled with grace, can leave everyone a future worth looking forward to.

Chapter 8

Getting Back to Life

The single mom life is hard. Harder than I ever knew, or imagined it would be. Many days I've felt like I'm standing in the ocean, being knocked over again and again by the waves that keep coming—and keep coming—and I'm not strong enough to push through them.

It's exhausting. Not only because this path is hard, but because we are likely doing it almost completely (if not completely) alone. And sometimes we wonder if that next wave is going to be the one that finally pulls us under. For good.

But, we have no choice.

We push through each day, doing all we can for our children. And as evening rolls in, we tuck our hearts, our feelings, and the dreams we once held into our back pocket believing that they are safer out of the way for now. That you and your tender heart are better with them hidden out of sight. Because even the slightest glimpse is too much at times. A reminder of everything you've lost. Of the pain. Of the unfairness of it all.

But, deep down, you know you need more.

With some distance between you and the starting point on this single motherhood path, you've done the hard work toward healing. You've grown. And you may have begun to dream—just a little.

By faith, I want you to be brave.

And I want you to do it knowing that many have gone before you the same way.

o Like Esther who stood up to save a nation . . . by faith.
o Like Hagar who trusted God after being banished . . . by faith.
o Like Ruth who trusted that her life would be redeemed . . . by faith.

Because courage to move forward isn't about us or what we can convince ourselves to do. Courage comes through faith. Knowing that there is One who is there with us in every battle. Holding us up against those waves. Not letting them knock us over. Then gently pushing us toward the shore to begin again.

It's your turn to take courage.

To stop listening to the booming voice in your head that tells you life is hard and you should just deal with the blows you've been given.

And listen instead to the voice that teaches that life can be beautiful, and fruitful, and redeemed.

"So be strong and courageous! Do not be afraid and do not panic before them. For the LORD your God will personally go ahead of you. He will neither fail you nor abandon you."
Deuteronomy 31:6 (NLT)

"This is my command—be strong and courageous! Do not be afraid or discouraged. For the LORD your God is with you wherever you go."
Joshua 1:9 (NLT)

A final word: Be strong in the Lord and in his mighty power.
Ephesians 6:10 (NLT)

You Can't Fight while Hiding

Through the years mothering my children, I've began to notice something about myself: when the going gets tough—and I mean really, really, tough—there's a chance you won't find me.

I have this really bad habit when things get to be too much, or when I just can't get past the things I'm hearing said about me.

I go into hiding.

Yes, I'm still taking the best care of my children that I can. Yes, I'm still running around town doing errands. But, beyond that—I go to my "place." The one that no one knows about. The one that feels safe, and non-judgy, and ready to accept me.

Don't we all have "that place" in our lives? Maybe it's your home and you go inside and make excuses as to why you don't really need to come out. Or maybe it's your car and you drive on and on until your gas light screams that you are getting to a final destination whether you like it or not. Or maybe you have a place in nature that calms you and reminds you for just a moment that you are more than a mom.

For me, it's a chair in my home.

A safe place where I feel secure. I depend on it waiting on me. And when life is overwhelming, and confusing, and just doesn't make sense at all, you'll likely find me there. And really, what's so bad about that? I mean, it's wonderful to have a place that can refill us, refresh us, right?

Except that it's also where I tend to get stuck.

Because sometimes retreating into our safety is a nice break. A place to recharge so we can hit the world again. But other times we go there with no plan to come out. We don't talk to anyone. We take care of the bare minimum responsibilities. We don't participate in life beyond the immediate.

Because the fear of hurting or being hurt more is scarier than the fear of being alone. And so we consciously choose to be alone.

The next step seems too painful to take. We can see it, just inches ahead, and know that it's going to be the thing that has the power to pull us back under. And after fighting to get out of our recent pit, we cling to our safe place now. Shuddering at the thought of edging anywhere close to the next step again.

But, sweet friend, you weren't called to hide from difficulties in this life, or as a mother. If the little bundles of energy filling up your laundry baskets and eating all of your hidden cookies aren't enough of a reminder, let this be:

"Have no fear of sudden disaster or of the ruin that overtakes the wicked, for the Lord will be at your side

and will keep your foot from being snared."
Proverbs 3:25-26(NIV)

That thing in your life you think is falling apart is still under the will of God.

That situation you think is hopeless is still under the control of God.

That person you feel is out to get you is still under the authority of God.

Your God.

The God who fights for you.

The God who will never leave you or forsake you.

The God who encourages you to take heart, and have courage, and try again. Because He can't heal what refuses to move. And there's nothing more He wants in life than a healthy daughter pushing toward the life He's called her to.

Are you ready?

When You're Still not Buying It

The year after my marriage fell apart was hands down the worst of my life.

Most days were a blur as I stumbled through them trying to contain my emotions and take care of my children. It was the pinnacle to a life of loss that seemed unbelievable, and undeserved, and just . . . unfair. It left me shaken, literally, as I noticed that I could no longer hold my drawing tools steady for my job as a textile designer. I felt like a shell of the person I'd once been. And I wondered if I even knew that girl anymore.

I took a year off from life—as much as I could. I still lived through it, but cut out anything "extra" from my days, knowing that I had some serious healing to do. Not only from my marriage, but from the loss of my family growing up, from being disowned by half my family, by a devastating job loss that financially destroyed me, and apparently every dream I ever held dear.

I clung to God's hand as if it was the sole thing that could pull me through. And it was. Day by day, He seemed to gently nudge me from my bed, push me along my tasks, and catch me when I crumbled into a pile of tears. He was so close—so close—that I felt the covering over me. The hovering, even. He was protecting His daughter when she could no longer stand up for herself, could no longer fight, could no longer move forward.

As the year went by, the burdens eased. The ache subsided a little. I began to poke my head above the bedsheets I hid under and wonder if there might be life outside the four walls I'd been hiding within.

After a season of loss or disappointment in your new or continued singleness, you'll see it too. That light just ahead. You'll long to reach for it; and when you do, you'll realize that it's life.

And it's yours for the taking.

A life of laughter instead of sorrow. Joy instead of mourning.

> *The Spirit of the Sovereign Lord is on me,*
> *because the Lord has anointed me*
> *to proclaim good news to the poor.*
> *He has sent me to **bind up the brokenhearted,***
> *to **proclaim freedom** for the captives*
> *and **release from darkness** for the prisoners,*
> *to proclaim the year of the Lord's favor*
> *and the day of vengeance of our God,*
> *to **comfort all who mourn,***
> *and provide for those who grieve in Zion—*
> ***to bestow on them a crown of beauty***
> ***instead of ashes,***
> ***the oil of joy***
> ***instead of mourning,***
> ***and a garment of praise***
> ***instead of a spirit of despair.***
> *They will be called oaks of righteousness,*
> ***a planting of the Lord***
> ***for the display of his splendor.***
>
> *They will rebuild the ancient ruins*
> ***and restore the places long devastated;***
> *they will renew the ruined cities*
> *that have been devastated for generations.*
> Isaiah 61:1-4 (NIV)

There will come a time when you stop going through the motions of caring for your children while ignoring your own obvious needs. You will decide that you're going to once again reach for something — not for your children, but for yourself.

For you. Just you.

And your loss will lift — ever so slightly.

And in that moment, God will rejoice, sweet friend. Because He longs to redeem the losses in your life. To hold your hand as you pull yourself up and move forward. As you look to Him for direction in the next step to take. Then have the courage to take it.

You can do it. Because He promises to restore what has been taken from you. If you'll just take the first step toward allowing Him.

"I will repay you for the years the locusts have eaten—the great locust and the young locust, the other locusts and the locust swarm— my great army that I sent among you."

Joel 2:25 (NIV)

Can we pray together over this?

Father God,

You alone know the struggles we face as single parents and the losses our hearts have suffered. We offer our hands up to You, knowing that You are there to take them and guide us gently back into the life You have planned for us. We open our hearts to You, longing for healing. And our minds, ready to be renewed. Cover us with Your love and protection as we begin to take the first steps toward restoring our lives and ourselves. Make Yourself known to us in real and tangible ways so that we become more aware each day of the fact that we are not alone on this path. We thank You, Lord, for healing, for new opportunities, and for Your gentleness of spirit that encourages us to move forward in our lives.

In Jesus' name we pray, Amen.

Getting Back to Life

It likely starts somewhere in our childhood: the first time we realize that we're really scared. Maybe it's sleeping without the nightlight for the first time. Or riding our bike without the training wheels. Or facing a bully alone.

We put on a brave face—because that's what strong people do—and suffer through something alone and scared knowing that we must because our parent's hand is just out of reach.

As we grow older, we perfect the skill. Through middle school when we feel like we have to say things we don't want to say. Through high school when we're pressured to do things we are certain we shouldn't. And even through college, our first job, or our first steps into parenting when how we handle scary situations become part of our success or failure.

THE SINGLE MOM CHALLENGE

We hone our brave faces until they mold perfectly. So perfectly, in fact, that we begin to forget they're there and they become our *fine* that helps us through life's painful moments.

- When our marriage is falling apart and we tell everyone we're *fine* because the pain is too much to talk about.
- When our health is struggling and we tell everyone we're *fine* so they won't feel burdened by us.
- When our financial situation is desperate and we tell everyone we're *fine* so we don't further embarrass ourselves.
- When our children are struggling and we tell everyone we're *fine* so we don't let them know that we think parenting is impossible at times.

Until one day we just can't lift the mask again. Our arms are suddenly incredibly weak, from years of holding it in place. We look around at those who would mock us (and maybe at some we know are mocking us) and decide that we don't care what they think anymore. We're sick to death of pretending and we let the mask drop.

Offering the rest of the world a look at what God already sees.

> **What is one thing you wish you'd handled differently as you started your single-mom journey?**
>
> *I wish I could have let go of a lot of the pain and anger sooner. I wish I had been able to see that I would NEVER have all the answers to my questions. I would never understand why he did what he did. I would never understand how he could go weeks without seeing his children. I would never understand why he felt he did not have to financially support them. I would never understand how he could do what he did to me. I would never understand how he went from somebody you knew and loved to somebody you had no idea who they were. These were questions that bothered me day in and day out. I constantly wondered why, how and what caused it. It took years to just say you know what...it is what it is...I don't know why and I never will. I needed to have faith that he would eventually see what he did to me and his children.*
>
> Angie, single mom of 2

It's in those moments of surrender—those broken moments where we feel we're just a shell of who we once were—that He finds us most precious, and that we open ourselves up to a life that's real. When we come to Him with the same passion we had for pretending to be brave and instead admit that we're scared to death—that we need Him to hold us—that we begin to feel again.

Because there is freedom in admitting we're scared.

In a world that competes through social media, and friendships that can't bear anything deeper than an excuse to get together and gossip, we're masters of the brave face.

In a society where we agree with things we don't believe for fear of being judged, and are scared to fight for things we do believe for fear of being outcasts, we're masters of the brave face.

Until we begin to see it for what it really is:

Nothing more than a barrier between what we have and what we really want.

A mask that keeps a wall between us and the people in our lives that we wish would dig deeper. People that won't know what we're going through unless we let that mask drop. And allow them the chance to see us— possibly for the first time.

And there's beauty in watching that mask fall. In seeing a friend give in so that God can have room to work. Beauty in seeing them realize that His hand is not so far away after all.

Ironically, that may be the bravest thing of all.

Sweet friend, if you are tired of holding that mask, I pray you will read this chapter and decide that NOW is the time to put it down—for good. Because life behind a mask is really no life at all is it? Life behind a mask is simply an act. A show we are putting on—for who? People we don't even know, or those who we are afraid will get too close when we are desperate for someone to see through it. For someone to see the real us struggling behind it.

It's time we put down the mask by breaking down the things that made us lift it to begin with. And we're starting with shame.

<u>Single Mom Challenge 12:</u>

You know that mask we talked about? Yeah. We're going to dig a little deeper with it. Because, you can't remove something you don't admit is there.

In this challenge I want you to consider how you have been hiding. What excuses you've used. Situations you've avoided. Lies you've told to protect yourself. Let's get a good picture of how far and deep and wide that mask is, so when we take it off, we can see how much light it's going to allow back into our lives.

Excuses I've used to avoid getting back to life:

_____

_____

_____

_____

_____

_____

Situations I've avoided:

_____

_____

_____

_____

_____

_____

Lies I've told to protect myself:

_____

_____

_____

_____

_____

Other ways I've hidden from life:

_____

_____

_____

_____

_____

Record these in your journal.

Living Shameless

One of the biggest shocks in my walk as a believer was how other believers reacted about my divorce. Not my personal, actual case of divorce. But how they would lump sum my divorce in with the world's divorces and assume that what I had done was unforgiveable (leaving my marriage) for the simple fact that "divorce is wrong" and "God hates divorce."

I discovered that there is a deep-held belief by some in the church that those who divorce will not be forgiven by God. Not only that, but that they are forever held in this sin of divorce, and then held captive in single status for the rest of their lives because remarrying another would be adultery.

They don't have to know your specific situation in order to draw conclusions. In fact, they probably won't even ask.

It surfaced in social media groups I was a part of. Someone would mention divorce and a stream of Bible verses condemning them would follow.

It surfaced in my friendships as I talked to other divorced moms and how they were singled out by people from their church with hateful emails or letters detailing how they would go to hell for committing adultery if they ever remarried.

But, before any of these things, it reminded me of a moment from early adulthood. A moment in college where someone I was close to (a seminary student) told me that my own mother was going to hell for adultery because she remarried after her divorce. He'd never met my mother, or knew anything behind the reasons for her divorce. He didn't even ask. And, I wasn't a believer at the time. You can imagine how close that brought me to God.

And so, a sour seed was planted in my heart that resurfaced as I realized that others (still) felt that way today. And because I believe that God forgives all sins of those who turn to Him—no matter what—I couldn't fathom this line of thinking:

Are the divorced unforgiveable?

I've been looking for answers on this because my single goal in life is to stay in the will of God. And, I fully believe that in some marriages, God calls people out of the marriage. Because we all know that marriages are often not what they seem from the outside. They can be full of sinful behavior that can only be escaped through divorce. And for an innocent in the marriage to suffer through a life of sin is not what God intends for anyone.

And there are only three people that will ever know the full truth of a marriage—the husband, the wife, and God.

Besides that, there are only three people whose business it is: the husband's, the wife's, and God's.

And so I wonder if these people who are quick to condemn, realize the pain that their victims are going through. And, not only that, but the additional pain they are causing–and the slippery slope they are walking as they lead another *away* from God based on their own self-righteousness.

Those of us who have suffered divorce know the devastating truth: the physical pain of being ripped apart from someone you once loved deeply is literally a tearing of the flesh from when two became one. And it feels like it. Physically, mentally, emotionally. To then have an outsider pour insults on the wound usually has no other effect than to turn that person away from God–in shame.

But, sweet friend, in the midst of that pain–when someone tries to fill you with shame, God is there too, offering to remove it. He still holds his hand toward the wretch that you may feel you are, and offers forgiveness and hope.

What Jesus doesn't offer, is shame.

Just like he didn't shame a Samaritan woman in John 4:

When Jesus asked her for a drink of water from the well, he told her "Everyone who drinks this water will be thirsty again, but whoever drinks the water I give them will never thirst. Indeed, the water I give them will become in them a spring of water welling up to eternal life."

Intrigued, she asked him for the water, to which he replied, "Go, call your husband and come back."

I imagine her lowering her head here as she said, "I have no husband."

But Jesus, in his great love and graciousness, said "You are right when you say you have no husband. The fact is, you have had five husbands, and the man you now have is not your husband. What you have just said is quite true."

He didn't belittle her. He didn't shame her. And, most importantly, he didn't then tell her that his offer of living water no longer applied to her. He didn't say, "I'm sorry. Since you had a husband and remarried another—much less four others—salvation is no longer available to you."

Instead, his acceptance of her led her to go out and tell others. She was so effective, that the Bible says that many came to believe in Jesus because of her testimony.

Because that's who Jesus is and what he can do in your life.

- o He is the God of the broken, of the wretch, of the sinner.
- o He is the God of the liar, the thief, the murderer.

- ○ He is the God of the depraved, the gluttonous, and the immoral.
- ○ He is the God who forgives a known criminal hanging on a cross beside Him, just moments before death strikes.

Because Jesus didn't come to this world to save those of us who lived perfect lives, following every rule written in the Bible. He didn't come to save those of us who know Him and know that we will make it into heaven because we do what He says and follow every little rule we've added to the mix. He didn't come to save those of us who have sinned in the past but will never make that mistake again in the future.

He came to this world to save the shamed.

Those who have fallen so far from perfect that they know—they know—that the only hope that they have in being a part of His life is to turn over every ounce of that broken life to Him. In the midst of our sins to turn to Him—tell Him we simply aren't good enough, and we know it—and then ask Him to love us anyway.

And He not only loves us, but sets us free. **Free to live shame-lessly for Him**. And that is a beautiful balm to an already broken heart. Is it not?

Because shame works against His greatest desires for you—to be in a close relationship with Him, and to tell others about Him too.

So, move on from your past—whatever that may be— knowing that you are forgiven. Completely. That you are to allow Him to lift that burden from your life, so that you can go out and tell others what He's done for you. I pray that you become so effective, that many will come to believe in Jesus because of your testimony. Because of the truth you live that nothing can hold you away from Him.

- o   Even after you sin again.
- o   Even after you hurt others.
- o   Even after your divorce.

Jesus shame-lessly forgave it all.

You do not have to live in shame. In fact, you should set yourself free from the burden of shame. Even if divorce is a sin, all sin except one— "If we confess our sins, He is faithful and righteous to forgive us our sins and to cleanse us from all unrighteousness." (1 John 1:9)—is covered by the cross. That one sin isn't divorce. It isn't even adultery. It's blasphemy against the Holy Spirit. (Mark 3:29) Jesus doesn't pick through our lives and pull out the sins He won't forgive and the ones He will. It is a blanket of forgiveness that spreads so wide we can't even catalogue it.

Jesus doesn't see things the way the world sees them. He looks beyond the surface — even beyond the sin — to see the person behind it. To see the heart.

He doesn't even interpret God's word the way that we do. In Luke, He speaks to the Pharisees about arguing over a specific sin. A sin listed in the 10 commandments that they had become so legalistic about that they could no longer use common sense.

One Sabbath day, a man with a deformed hand was in the synagogue where Jesus was teaching. The religious teachers and Pharisees there began to watch Jesus closely to see if He would break the commandment of resting on the Sabbath. But Jesus, who knew what they were thinking, called the man to him, and healed him.

He said to them:

"I have a question for you. Does the law permit good deeds on the Sabbath, or is it a day for doing evil? Is this a day to save life or to destroy it?" (Luke 6:1-11)

The last part of the verse strikes me. "Is this a day to save a life or to destroy it?" By not healing the man's hand, his life may not have been literally destroyed. He probably would have gone home and continued on in his daily life just as he had before. But, by Jesus choosing to heal this

LAURA POLK

man, by touching this man He touched every aspect of His life. By offering him physical healing, healing would come in other areas of his life as he became a sold-out believer for Jesus. By looking at the law, and seeing how it was being twisted to hurt the people it intended to protect, Jesus chose to see the man that would have been most affected by it—and offered healing.

Jesus didn't come to this world to save marriage as an institution. Nowhere in the Bible does it say that Jesus came to save marriage, or even families. Jesus is concerned about individuals to the point that He states that some will lose family members when they come to the faith. He came to save specific people. You. Me. Our ex. Our children. Separate from each other. Separate from the institutions we participate in. His overarching goal is to pull us into relationship with Him.

And He won't let anything stand in His way of that:

o   Not the Pharisees in our life
o   Not how we see ourselves
o   Not the boxes people put us in while hiding their own sin (haughty eyes, self-righteousness, lying, gluttony, etc.)
o   Not divorce

If so, He would have walked right by the woman at the well. Why save her when she was irredeemable? He would have left the man in the synagogue crippled. Why care about him when the commandment clearly stated rest? He saw the people behind the situations and made a judgment call of the law that was clearly being twisted away from the heart of what God intended.

He came for you too.

Single Mom Challenge 13:

Shame is a life-stealer. It can keep us isolated from everything and everyone that might help us move forward. And once we allow it in our hearts and minds, it's hard to get rid of. But, that's what we're going to start here. We're going to lay that "thing" out on the table. That word someone spoke to you. That thought that keeps flickering through your head. Whatever it is that makes you feel shamed, we're going to expose it to the Light. The light of day, and the Light of our God. And we're going to ask Him to remove it from us so that we can move forward toward the life He's planned for us instead.

List the "things" that have caused shame to rear its ugly head in your life:

1. _____

2. _____

3. _____

4. _____

5. _____

Take a long look at that list, sweet friend. Mull over it. Consider how it has caused you to retreat in life. How it has held you back at times and pulled you back to the pit you've just climbed out of.

When you're ready, call on God. Move through the list, one-by-one, and ask Him to remove it from you. Tell Him you are giving it over to Him, and you're choosing to walk in His light instead.

Record these in your journal.

Chapter 9

When You Mess it All Up

I'm a woman just like you.

I do my best to raise my children. To excel at my job. To take care of my home. To be a good friend, daughter, sister, and aunt.

I'm also a Christian.

For some reason, that last fact seems to trump everything when I reach my breaking point of having enough. As if all the things that happen in the life of a Christian are somehow negated the day they've had enough. The day they lose their cool. Even a little.

But sometimes what others intend for harm can be used for good in God's economy. Sometimes our breaking point can be a clarifying point in our faith. The thing that solidifies it for us.

I spent the first three years after my marriage ended living in fear. I was stalked. And harassed. And berated on a daily basis. I was humiliated. And lied about. And taunted at every step. My property and the property of those I cared most about had been damaged. The other women in my life had been targeted. And my children suffered emotionally to no end.

All to show me that my ex wanted to harm me more than anything else in life:

o   More than he wanted a healthy relationship with his children.
o   More than he wanted to be an upstanding person in our small community.
o   More than he wanted to stay on the right side of the law.
o   More than he wanted to move on from his past.

Maybe you can understand how someone like me — someone much like you — would reach a breaking point. That I would fight back. That I would send a scathing, curse-word filled message to this person on behalf of my children, simply trying to protect them.

Being Christian doesn't equal being perfect.

Far from it, in fact. Because being a Christian often means that you are the most authentic version of yourself. That you take off the masks and begin to live a transparent life that honors God. Or, I should say, that is trying to honor God.

Even when you mess up.

As I sat in court again after sending that letter, after the prior three years of living in fear, I overheard a pack of lawyers debating my status as a Christian because of my choice words. As I watched them and the person who wanted to harm me poke each other in the side over the idea that I was a fraud, as I listened to a DA imply that I was doing things out of sheer ridiculousness instead of actually trying to stop someone from physically harming me . . .

I was stunned.

As if there was anything left to be done to me that hadn't already been done by my ex and the court system that favored him.

Because regardless of what I was going through, and how I reacted, despite the lies being told and the victim status I begrudgingly held, I was first and foremost a woman of God.

Despite how I acted. Despite my failure to be gracious. Despite feeling like I was no longer worthy of that title.

Even after I failed.

Even when I didn't feel like I was.

Even when my heart and mind were so broken and fragmented in my circumstances that I could barely remember Him.

Even when I hit "enough" and cursed at my accusers.

The beauty in it all, the beauty that they couldn't see as they passed my letter around, leering at me and laughing so I would hear them—is that there was nothing they could do or say to change that truth.

No amount of poking fun at my expense. No amount of telling me I'm not a Christian because I'm not acting like a godly woman when I misstep. No amount of shaming me, or scaring me, or threats to expose me can change that.

I am a woman of God.

And so are you.

We can cling to the fact that our God was a man of strength and character. A man who fought for those who were wronged. A man who showed His anger. A man who taught that His followers would all be mocked at His expense. A man who picked up those who made the most heinous mistakes in life, brushed them off, and asked them to follow Him anyway.

That He fights for me, when I can no longer gather the strength to fight for myself.

That He loves me no matter what I say or do.

That He is my biggest supporter as my accusers face me.

And He is yours as well.

I know that you have had your faith questioned in an attempt to tear it down.

I know that you've been out there in a boat beside me, riding through this hurricane.

I know that you've reached out for help only to be shamed, or treated like a bothersome gnat, or simply ignored.

You've reached your breaking point like I did, only to then have your accusers try to steal the last remaining thing you are clinging to in your life—your place alongside God.

But, they are wrong.

They can't take it from you. In fact, their taunting builds your treasure in heaven. Their lies champion God to your side. Their attempts will never win over you. Because our God won't back away like the others in our life. He won't believe the lies like the others in our life. He won't leave us in this mess like the others in our life.

He is ours and we are His.

No matter what.

Because we are women of God.

We can't let our mistakes lead us to believe that we don't still deserve that. And we can't hide from life when—not if—we mess up.

<u>Single Mom Challenge 14:</u>

It's never too late to start anew. We serve the God of second-chances. The God who sees us for who we truly are. The God who loves us so outrageously that He sacrificed His life so that we might be with Him in eternity. He is gracious. And forgiving. And everything we can't imagine we are worthy of. But we are. You are His daughter. And there's nothing you can do to make Him stop loving you or stop wanting you in His life.

There are times when we need to get real with God. To talk about the hard topics. The things we've hidden from Him. So that we can put it behind us and move forward in grace.

If you've backtracked, or slid, or whatever you want to label it, bring it to Him now. You don't need to write it down. Because as soon as you talk to Him about it, ask for His forgiveness, and earnestly choose to move away from it, He accepts. You start anew with Him. And you can move forward with a clear conscience.

Talk to Him now.

When you are done, sign your name here:

_____

How a Bad Day is Born

It starts something like this:

- o You walk into church on Sunday and notice the woman from your last Bible study is looking at you weird.
- o Throughout the service, you can't get her off of your mind. Why would she look at you like that? It had to be what you said about the evils of tofu. She looks Vegan.
- o You can't concentrate at all. In fact, you've just noticed that she is sitting three rows ahead to your right and you're pretty sure she's looking at you out of the corner of her eye.
- o She's judging you. Yes.
- o Like she's never had a cookie. You think about pulling a pack of cookies from your purse and eating them right then just to irritate her.
- o How dare her. Who does that in church? I mean, looking at people??
- o You miss the entire sermon as you watch her, seething.
- o But when they call for prayer, you decide to do the right thing: You pray she gets that chip off her shoulder.

o   As the service ends, you watch as she gathers her
    things and walks toward the door. She is smiling at
    everyone she passes. Then, she purposefully gets in
    front of you. And walks. Ridiculously. Slow.
o   It's all a plot to make you angry. But, you're not
    going to fall for it.
o   At the exit, she notices you behind her, holds the
    door for you and smiles.
o   She's like a mastermind, that one.
o   You just give her the eye—the same dirty eye she
    gave you earlier—and walk on without comment.
o   You're not going to let her ruin *your* day.

Ahem.

Not that I think like that.

Okay, yeah. I do sometimes.

The truth is that negative thinking is . . . well . . . sticky,
isn't it?

We start with a tiny thought that crosses our mind.
Then other thoughts seem to stick to it as it rolls through
our head, much like a snowball effect. By the time we've
really rolled it over and over, it has turned into a huge
ordeal that will probably never happen, and we've
allowed the negative thought to take over us—and likely
ruined our mindset for the rest of the day.

I'll admit, throughout my gig as a single mother, it's been trending in my life. I've gone from looking for the silver lining, to waiting for the sky to fall. I find myself on the negative side of the fence way more often than I'd like to admit. If truth be told, I've put in a pool and spent hours sitting over there ruminating.

It can happen to the best of us. Especially after a long season of difficulty. We begin to expect the worst, because—hey—that's all we've seen in quite a while. So much so, that we forget that the good often comes the same way. As the small things that annoy us build up in other areas of our lives, we can no longer see the good for the tall tales of bad we keep spinning.

But, I'm moving on from that negativity now. Not only because I know it's toxic for me, but because it's even more toxic for my children.

I don't want my kids taking on this sticky habit of negativity.

Because there is great power in the way we allow ourselves to think. Taking a negative angle on life is easy, because it's how the world lives. It's all around us. Hey—everyone is doing it. **But, we are called to live differently.**

Don't copy the behavior and customs of this world, but let God transform you into a new person by changing the way you think.

Then you will learn to know God's will for you, which is good and pleasing and perfect.

Romans 12:2 (NLT)

We have to fight to see the good in this world. Even more so, is the fight **to be the good** in this world.

But, that's where God leads us.

And now, dear brothers and sisters, one final thing. Fix your thoughts on what is true, and honorable, and right, and pure, and lovely, and admirable. Think about thinks that are excellent and worthy of praise.

Philippians 4:8 (NLT)

Because, at the end of the day, we hold a lot of power in our children's lives. The power to hurt, or heal. The power to build up, or tear down. The power to choose the positive, or the negative.

And I'm positive we hold the same power in our own.

Single Mom Challenge 15:

We're moving on from our past, sisters, and focusing on the positive future ahead. List 20 positive things in your life right now. They're there. :

1. _____

2. _____

3. _____

4. _____

5. _____

6. _____

7. _____

8. _____

9. _____

10. _____

11. _____

12. _____

13. _____

14. _____

15. _____

16. _____

17. _____

18. _____

19. _____

20. _____

Transfer these to your journal.

When You Find the Chip is Still There

Sometimes we think we are moving along, healing nicely, and ready for the future when we realize that we've still got a little further to go.

Several years into single motherhood, life was finally getting back on track for me. I felt healthy, had a positive outlook, and was growing in my faith again. But, my ex was continuing to make things difficult on occasion. Being a practitioner of what I preach, I went to a Christian Counselor to talk about ways to manage his attempts to disrupt my life.

At this point, I had relegated my ex to email only contact. So, the only way for him to "get" to me was if I purposefully went into my junk folder (where I had his emails automatically sent) and read them. Most days, I avoided that folder like the plague. But, if I sensed something unhealthy going on between him and my kids, it was the first place I checked. If he was sending me hate-mail, it was typically a good indicator of things going on with them.

My counselor and I had recently tried Cognitive Processing Therapy (CPT). It's something that's used with those who have suffered PTSD, which my counselor believed I had as a result of the continued harassment and stalking the prior three years. In CPT, you essentially learn how to evaluate and change your thought process regarding traumatic events so that you no longer feel the stress, fear, or anxiety associated with it.

The idea was to take the "trigger," which for me was hateful emails, and begin to address it so that it no longer held the power it did previously. And it was working.

After a few sessions, as I visualized the emails, I no longer tensed up or felt an overwhelming sense of anxiety. In fact, as I visualized one particularly harmful email, it was as if I gained control over it and it began to slip away from my field of view. To the point that I could no longer see what it said.

During our last session, I visualized the email to the point that it slipped away. I could no longer see it, and there was no stress or dread involved.

That's when I felt God come to my side.

He surrounded me as I stood against this thing in my life that was harming me. I was completely enveloped by Him—except for my left arm. Which I then noticed had a chip of wood on it that slanted at a weird angle.

My counselor ended the session shortly after and stated that he believed the chip had been placed there by God as if to say to my ex: Don't touch this. Don't touch her again.

But, I knew better.

The chip was mine.

And what it really represented was my defiance and an unwillingness to bend toward God as I was healing—because I'd felt hurt by Him. It made me realize that though I'd come a long way and was rebuilding my faith and able to look back and see how far God had brought me, I still was hurt by what I felt like He let me endure.

As time has moved on even from that point, I've begun to learn more and more about how this time in my life is being used by God to shape me, my children, and my future. It's been a crucial time for what I feel like God is calling me toward in the future—even though I don't fully understand what that is yet.

My point is this:

Just when we think we are healed and free from what was so hard for so long, there is often much to be learned from it.

Don't skip that step.

As you move forward, you don't need to drag the past behind you like a wounded leg. That will get you nowhere. But also, you don't need to haze over what you've gone through and blindly push forward without looking around it and through it to see how God worked. That's what our journals are for, sweet friends.

It's so important to look at where we've been, think through it, and learn from it. Otherwise, we are sure to make similar choices that will lead us to a similar path we were on when we arrived at single motherhood. We don't want that, do we? We're taking this opportunity we've been given and using it to dramatically change our future outcomes.

But it takes a concerted effort on our part. A willingness and drive to seek where He is in it, how He walked us through it, and what He wants us to learn from it.

Continue to open your heart to the wisdom He wants to share with you. To the ways He wants to show you that He used what you went through not only for your own good in the long run, but for His Glory.

What a waste to experience all that we have experienced and miss the story of faith that He walked through with us.

<u>Single Mom Challenge 16:</u>

When we are going through something—in the very thick of it—it's hard to see what God is doing. That's what I hope your journals will help you with. Over the next weeks and months, I pray that you will continue to pour your heart out to Him there. That you will make notes of Him moving. And that you will begin to consider how what you've gone through, and what He is doing will change your future path for the better.

Set a goal for your journal. Whatever you feel is best.

Write it here:

_____

_____

_____

_____

_____

_____

_____

_____

_____

_____

_____

_____

Transfer that goal to the front of your journal.

The End You Didn't See Coming

It was one of those days where everything was fine just 24 hours earlier. I blindly went along believing that life was finally settling down. That a new normal was just up ahead. That no matter what was happening around me; I would eventually get through the chaos and to the other side.

Until I received another family court notice in the mail. Another sign that my ex was determined to continue to make this road as difficult as possible. Just another reminder of how alone I was as a single mom.

And I realized that I was falling again.

Or maybe I should say failing again.

Because that's what it felt like.

Several years into life as a single mom, I still wasn't sure I had a handle on it. There were still moments of deep grief for what my children faced. There were moments of incredible fear. Moments of pure panic at how on earth I'd do it all, provide it all, and manage it all.

Before I was a single mom, I was the mom who could do it all with ease.

But, I realized that the life I was leading was—in all honesty—a lie I was convincing myself to believe. When reality hit, I felt as if I'd been sucker punched. This too-trusting girl took a long, hard look at her actual life and realized that it was not what she was making it seem to the rest of the world. To her extended family. To herself.

She was holding it together by so many tiny threads, manipulating each one just so, that she realized if she let even one go, it would all become a tangled, matted mess.

And that's what it became.

There are moments that I'm ashamed that's all I have to offer to anyone: a mess. And can I just tell you something? There aren't many takers to walking alongside someone whose life looks like that.

But, there is One who has walked it from the very beginning. Even when I couldn't admit what He was showing me was true. Even in the deep grief that followed me choosing to end my marriage. And I've trusted Him as He's led me into these murky waters that I feared. Fear still. Because I trusted that in the end, there was something better that He had for me.

- o   A life that wasn't filled with lies and cover-ups.
- o   A life that wasn't consumed with fear of what would happen next.
- o   A life that could allow others in.
- o   A life in which I could finally open my heart to those around me.

Sometimes your something better may look like the thing you fear the most. The thing you never, ever, in a million years, wanted. Maybe it's not even the path God originally intended for you to take. But it's the path God needs you on now in order to get to the end-place He planned all along.

I want that something better. And I bet you do too.

Having to choose a path that scares us is often the thing that keeps us stuck on the wrong road for so long. We'll do anything to convince ourselves that we are happy on the wrong path. That we can manage the wrong path. That God actually prefers us on the wrong path.

Sometimes your something better isn't getting what you thought you wanted. It's what God had in mind. What is truly better for you instead.

And you just have to blindly trust Him to lead you to it.

> I will say of the Lord, "He is my refuge and my fortress,
> my God, in whom I trust."
>
> Psalm 91:2 (NIV)

For the first time in probably my entire life, I'm learning how to let people love me.

And it's hard.

I struggle not to bend over backwards to make it easier on others who are against me. I struggle to face reality head on and not gloss it over as I tend to do. And I struggle not to tuck my head under the covers or run with full force away from what is up ahead.

And I do so only because it's God's hand that's led me here. Regardless of how I feel about where I am, or how I came to be here—make no mistake: I am His, and He has led me here.

Some days, that's the only thing I have to cling to. But, even on those hard days, it's so much better than clinging to the lies I was gripping onto with dear life before. *Because God is on this path with me. Ahead of me. Beside me. Behind me.*

Even if the starting line is not where I imagined I'd begin, the end will be *so much better.*

And so will yours.

LAURA POLK

THE SINGLE MOM CHALLENGE

What Other Single Moms Want You to Know:

I asked single moms in my ministry to answer this one question: *What would you say to encourage another single mom of faith on her journey?*

Do you. If one night you can't get to the dishes, it's okay. Don't be so hard on yourself. You are doing great and in your children's eyes, you are Wonder Woman. Learn to say no. Your time is precious. Make moments count. Dance in the kitchen. Have tickle fights. Sit and watch a movie with your children on the couch. Play Barbies. Color. Laundry can wait. Most importantly, understand that although single parenting was not part of what you planned for you or your children's lives, it's your reality. For whatever reason, God closed one door to open another. During this time, you'll realize you have strength that you never knew you possessed. All to be witnessed by your greatest fans—your kiddos.

Cristie, single mom of 3

Stop beating yourself up about your past, you're doing a brilliant job and your kids will thank you for it one day.

Linda, single mom of 4

God is near the broken hearted. Hold tight as He takes you on an amazing journey of building your faith!

Dena, single mom of 3

God is GOOD! Through all the dark days, He has BEEN THERE! Provision, a job, rent money, the car continuing to run for 15 years and still going (please, Lord, 1 more year). College tuition, school clothes, you name it, He is faithful. I'm the LAST person that ever wanted to be a single mom. Yet my youngest is a senior in high school, and even though we are still having struggles, now I KNOW we will not be abandoned by Him-EVER!

Ranee, single mom of 4

I know this is harder than you expected and you feel alone. Please know that God will be as close to you as you ask Him to be.

Kathleen, single mom of 1

This is only one moment. The Lord has a plan for you and your children.

Kristina, single mom of 2

The journey we are on may be hard, faced with a lot of limitations, and you feel you are constantly running on EMPTY. But knowing no matter what challenges you face big or small, or not knowing what tomorrow may bring or the things that you don't understand, know without fail who IS holding our hand is the only assurance we can get through anything. What an Awesome God He is.

Fahina single mom of 5

Philippians 4:13 is my number one verse that got me through hard times. I've held onto it by the tips of my fingers & showed my children how our Heavenly Father is there even in the middle of life's storms.

Christy, single mom of 2

Hold on to hope in Jesus. His light is found in the darkest points of your journey.

Angela, single mom of 2

As long as you place God in the center of your life to help you parent your children everything will not be as hard as it seems.

Ana, single mom of 2

Focus on the good in everyday, no matter how small it may seem. Slowly shift your mindset to one of gratefulness and joy. It is hard to find joy. During these difficult times take time to accept the offers of help from others without guilt. There will be a time when you can pay it forward. During these times, focus your efforts and energies on the things that are within your power to change. You cannot change other people, only how you choose to react to them. You cannot change your finances, you can only change how you spend your money. Allow yourself to feel sad or angry, set a timer for 10 minutes and get it out. When the timer goes off, stop wallowing, pray, and get on with your life. Keep making baby steps to move forward.

Covey, single mom of 3

I'm so thankful now that God allows (difficult) things to happen. Who I am right now is because of God's plan for me, and I know I will never lose that faith because He always had wonderful plans in store for us.

Crizzysanti, single mom of 2

Though it may be hard, the best thing to do is WAIT for God's timing in relationships. For healing. For the next time. Wait and seek God.

Kristen, single mom of 3

Entrusting the children God gave you is a one-time decision and a process. Drink plenty of water. Feed on God's word, even when you don't think you need it. Have snacks ready in the car to curb outbursts. Stop beating up yourself. You can't do everything you want to do. You are only one person--and that's okay. If you are a believer of Christ, you can pass down a legacy of faith in Jesus to your children. Get sleep. Dance in the kitchen with your kids. You are not defined by your marital status...or the behavior of your children, be it good or not so good.

Elizabeth, single mom of 3

There may be times when it's overwhelming, and you see only your own footprints. That's when you're at your strongest because God is carrying you! While you're waiting for the storm to pass, God takes your hand and gives you the strength you need to dance in the rain.

Amanda, single mom of 1

THE SINGLE MOM CHALLENGE

Pray, pray, pray! Don't run away from the Lord and your faith. This journey is long and hard but you are not alone. The Lord is with you. He has not forgotten you. Things will get better. Hugs sweet sisters,

Jess, single mom of 2

Cling to the Lord. Know that your worth and value is not reflective based on what your husband thinks of you. The Word tells us of our great value and worth through Christ. He knows our hurt and our pain. We are not alone.

Jennifer, single mom of 3

Trust God still has a great plan and purpose for your life and your children. Trust Him! He loves you so much and He loves your children. He does really work everything together for your good. He opens up doors no man can shut! He has provided for us and kept us through the good and bad times! Love you sister! Hold on.

Tammy, single mom of 3

It's not easy but it's worth it. Ask for help if possible and don't beat yourself up for needing it.

Sharon, single mom of 2

You are not alone. I know the days are hard, lonely and frustrating. But you are not alone. You truly do have a Heavenly Father who loves you and is there for you. Never forget that.

Kelly, single mom of 3

201

Keep your eyes on Him! Don't look down, look up.

Emma, single mom of 2

About the Author

LAURA POLK is a writer, speaker, and textile designer residing in North Carolina with her three children. Since becoming a single mom, her passion to minister to this group has led her to encourage successful single mom living through her online ministry and The Christian Single Mom community on Facebook.

For more on Laura, visit www.laurapolk.com